Creative Partnerships: Librarians and Teachers Working Together

By Lesley S. J. Farmer

PROFESSIONAL GROWTH SERIES

A Publication of THE BOOK REPORT & LIBRARY TALK
Professional Growth Series

Published by Linworth Publishing, Inc.
480 East Wilson Bridge Road, Suite L
Worthington, Ohio 43085

Copyright © 1993 by Linworth Publishing, Inc.

Series Information:

From The Professional Growth Series

ISBN 0-938865-13-7

5 4 3 2 1

Table of Contents

Introduction

Librarians and teachers share many common goals and philosophies. They are caring professionals who, of course, want the best for their students. This book helps these educators learn to work together to maximize the benefits of professional partnerships. It begins with a discussion of the need for partnerships, the benefits and obstacles in creating them, then moves on to explain how to develop successful partnerships. Successive chapters enumerate how to structure joint planning and provide tips on teaching information literacy. Ideas for joint programs and services such as events and contests, displays, publications and other documents, and school-generated information are developed. Computer issues are addressed. The final chapters deal with collection development and maintenance, joint fund-raising and evaluation, particularly of the partners. Selected readings from THE BOOK REPORT give teachers and librarians further inspiration to develop meaningful educational partnerships.

About the Author

Lesley S. J. Farmer is the Library Director of the San Domenico School in San Anselmo, California. She has extensive experience as a school librarian, as a young adult and children's specialist in public libraries, and as a library science instructor, most recently at San Jose State University. Dr. Farmer is the author of a number of articles and books on librarianship.

Section 1

Why Develop Partnerships?

It's the end of the year. The classroom teachers have left. I'm doing the book inventory, rediscovering little-used treasures. "Wow! Mrs. N could have really used this! The religion class would have had a great time doing a project using these books! Why don't the physics students use these materials more often; they keep saying how hard it is to understand the concepts." That's when I wish for more and stronger librarian-teacher partnerships.

A Little History

While *Information Power* has been loudly touted recently and schools are waking up to its stated mission, the concept of librarian-teacher partnership has been around for a long time. By 1974 *Audiovisual Instruction* magazine had established instructional program development as part of a school librarian's function. I remember giving talks 15 years ago about librarians and teachers working together. And groundwork on such partnering had been laid years before. In fact, several states use the title "library teacher" or its equivalent to emphasize the teaching role of the school librarian. (I will use the classic term "librarian" to denote these important instructors and will use the term "teacher" to denote classroom teachers, mindful of the "librarian" who said he had the largest classroom in the school!)

Why Isn't It Happening?

One reason is that teachers don't know or don't see the need for librarian-teacher partnering. Few teacher credential programs include team-teaching models, particularly including librarians as the collaborators. High school teachers, in particular, tend to be credentialed in a specific subject area, and they consider themselves experts in their field. How could a librarian know more about their subject than they—how could a librarian tell them how to teach their courses?

During in-services where teachers have a choice of workshops to attend, they may shy away from the topic of partnerships with librarians, thinking: "Oh, it's for librarians, not me." When I spoke at an International Reading Association conference about this issue, of the 26 attendees, 25 were librarians—only one was a classroom teacher. What is the result? Librarians talk among themselves, often complaining about lack of teacher participation, and teachers remain ignorant of the help awaiting them.

Another reason for the lack of teacher-librarian collaboration is that teachers may see partnerships as more work. Again, in higher grades, teachers feel constrained by rigorous content demands, and think that "library time" cuts into their teaching time. What they don't see is that investing time in information literacy or library skills will enable students to learn more effectively. Furthermore, those processing skills lead to lifelong learning.

Teachers also know that working with another person can "slow them down." Particularly if a teacher has a course that works well for him/her, there is little motivation to change it. Changing tactics and developing closer professional working relationships require extra time and effort. The payback may be slow in coming, too long for some teachers. So another basic issue is change.

Another issue is the perception of the library. If the school considers the library to be a warehouse of materials rather than an instructional learning center, then activity related to the library will be limited to warehouse type functions: storing and retrieving items. If the administrators see the librarian as a clerk, then they will not be likely to support the librarian's efforts to help develop curriculum. A definite dichotomy still exists between operations and policy-making, and many librarians are relegated to the former status.

However, the "blame" cannot be laid just on the teachers' shoulders. Librarians too may lack perspective. They may have been trained before a partnership approach was emphasized. They may have been trained for another library specialty, such as public librarian. They may have been classroom teachers who wanted to "escape" the drudgery of grading and coursework (those folks are in for a surprise).

Some librarians may be reluctant to initiate partnerships with teachers. They might be the first ones in their school to use that approach or may not have the administrator's backing. Some librarians may have tried a couple of times with disappointing results and decided that partnering isn't worth the trouble and the rejection. And some might not feel comfortable with the partnership process: finding lessons that lend themselves to collaborative planning, scheduling time to operate, choosing a means of instruction, and agreeing on ways to evaluate results. In short, librarians may be fearful or uncomfortable about change in their surroundings or themselves.

Particularly as budgets have decreased, librarians may share the teachers' concern about high work demands and little time to accomplish them. Librarians may have no support staff or may be part-timers themselves. When prioritizing tasks, librarians may have to concentrate on collection development and maintenance rather than partnering, since instruction can be done by other teachers.

Finally, some librarians really don't *want* to partner. They may like to be independent, they may be burned out, or they may like just the technical part of librarianship. Hopefully, those people will have others on their staff to carry out active partnerships.

Why Partner?

Partnerships are important because students deserve the very best education possible and they need to see good models of education. Particularly in a learning community, which the school should model, all people involved in that community should be learning and sharing with each other. Students need to see librarians and teachers working together so they will be more motivated and equipped to work with their peers and with adults. Students need to see extensive, high-quality library services and programs so they will demand and support similar standards in other libraries for themselves and their children.

Certainly, teachers and librarians have needs that each can meet with their own skills. In fact, teachers and librarians can be seen working in parallel, each planning and implementing the same kinds of learning activities that could be accomplished in tandem. It is assumed that both want to teach students, and that they possess certain skills and knowledge to perform that duty. It is also assumed that they have limited time and resources. Teachers possess content knowledge about their field, be it an academic discipline or the workings of a specific age group. Teachers also have personal knowledge about their students, especially if they teach one group all day, every day. Librarians possess knowledge and skills about information and ways to process it: locating and accessing it, evaluating and selecting it, interpreting it, synthesizing and organizing it, and sharing it. In addition, librarians know students in a different context: as readers and helpers and wonderful young personalities. Librarians may also be considered generalists, in contrast to specialized teachers. They have an overview of the entire curriculum, and work with all children. This breadth of knowledge helps students bridge their learning from one discipline to another and from one grade to another. So, together, teachers and librarians can complement each other and provide a richer and broader base for student learning. In the process, they can learn from each other and develop themselves professionally.

What Makes It Happen?

Librarians and teachers have the foundation for building strong partnerships. Since learning occurs throughout life, many opportunities exist to develop skills and confidence to expand and sustain librarian-teacher partnerships. This book is a start. Educational literature and workshops offer more chances to gather ideas to implement. The main requisite is a mind open to change and ready to share learning. Librarians need to get out into the rest of the school by attending departmental meetings, participating on committees, conducting workshops, and instructing in classrooms. And they need to communicate that they are ready to go that extra mile.

Librarians exemplify school involvement when they take on course duties in addition to their librarianship repertoire. Some act as sponsors of classes or clubs. They may be after-school athletic coaches, literally out on the field helping students grow day and night. Of course, not every librarian need be a sports coach, and a balance must be struck—assuming too many extra duties may endanger the quality of library service. But as coaches work with other adults, so do librarians and teachers "coach" together so their students can reach their individual goals.

Librarians need to be proactive educators, working with teachers to develop the best learning opportunities possible: maximizing material *and* human resources. The first step starts within one's self: to feel confident about one's work and to want to share that knowledge, for the sake of students. The second step is to initiate meaningful professional relationships and to work with other educators. Perhaps the third step will be for librarians to share this book with teachers so they can gain perspective and get ideas for ways to enter into successful partnerships.

Section 2
Developing Effective Partnerships

How many times have you been in the middle of a project (maybe troubleshooting a computer) when a classload of students entered the library buzzing with questions? That's the first time you find that the teacher has assigned them oral reports on South American countries: indigenous people, colonialism, current political system, and current economic trends. Noticing the teacher is nowhere in sight, you grab an assignment sheet, gather the students to the reference area, and quickly give them some guidance. While you are glad that the students are using the library constructively, you sigh about the teacher. Not a great partnership.

Sometimes when the words "partner" or "resource-based learning" arise, the underlying principle is short-shrifted. A partnership is more than students using library books; it's a conscious, collaboratively planned activity that involves content, delivery, and evaluation pieces.

David Loertscher's book *Taxonomy of the School Library Media Program* (Libraries Unlimited, 1988) describes the continuum of teacher-librarian relationships, and emphasizes the active role of the librarian needed for meaningful planning and partnership building. Of course, a prerequisite is to operate the library competently, meeting required collection and facilities standards. Once that goal is accomplished, the following steps constitute a framework for establishing and maintaining teacher-librarian partnerships:

☐ Use the informal system:
- Attract teachers.
- Meet with teacher groups (i.e., departments, grade levels, core groups)
- Plan and implement one-time activities (lessons, events, displays, documents) with a few teachers.

☐ Legitimize structures:
- Formalize partnerships by getting administrative support.
- Establish a library board or steering committee.
- Join committees.

□ Integrate and expand the system:
  - Develop a range of library services: information literacy goals and objectives, programs and events, displays, documents.
  - Target a group of teachers for full-fledged partnerships.
  - Provide in-service workshops with teachers.
  - Establish a school-wide partnership plan.

The remainder of the section discusses this framework in depth.

Use the Informal System

Attract teachers:

Developing teacher-librarian partnership requires a professional level of trust. Both parties must be viewed as competent, dependable, and open to communication. In a school, most people are first perceived in terms of their educational function: do they know their job? The assumption is that to be hired, one must possess a certain body of knoweldge. However, it's the workaday behavior that is observed. Unfortunately, some people never seem to transcend their job title; they aren't perceived as unique individuals. A personal, emotional bond must be established, and that connection must be honest and real. If that initial bond of trust does not occur, then subsequent encounters will remain limited in scope and depth. There's no magic about trust-building; it's a matter of conscious self-assessment--and an eagerness to learn about other people and enjoy them. A natural openness creates an inviting atmosphere that will attract both faculty and students.

So the librarian is a decent educator and an OK person; what does the library have to offer the teacher? The "Attract Mode," a part of public relations, has kicked in. In a way, librarians need to advertise their "wares." Now some people may get nervous when thinking about advertising. Visions of subversive propaganda come to mind. Rather, advertising can be considered as a way of making people aware of services and product. Education is the goal. And that's laudable.

Genuine caring and attractiveness generate a like atmosphere in the library. Do teachers feel welcome in the library? Does a spirit of active learning exist there? Is there a spot for teachers to work or to relax? Is there a sense of order and calm that invites teachers to explore? For many, the library is a safe haven in a chaotic world, a stimulating homebase where students and teachers can take intellectual and creative risks without threat. Does that atmosphere prevail in the library? In Section 9, Dian Ziller lists "35 good reasons to send a student to the library," demonstrating the benefits of a positive library setting.

Beyond an attractive atmosphere, the library must offer a clear "menu" of resources and services. I've seen brochures about libraries listing collection numbers, square footage, and staff. Not very interactive. Rather, the library should be described in terms of the users' active needs: exploring careers, making classroom transparencies, getting sample driver's tests, finding diagrams to aid in a dissection project, holing up in a quiet corner to read a mystery. The more specific examples cited, the more real the library becomes.

One clever way to make teachers aware of the library is to develop a survey (Oh, no, not another survey!). Simply asking the teachers how often they use the library for different purposes subtly communicates what the library has to offer. Of course, the survey should be short and professional; that initial image is as important on paper as it is in person. The survey results also let the librarian know which areas need to be emphasized. That valuable input helps establish direction for building partnerships. (A sample teacher survey is provided at the end of this section.)

Basically, the librarian tries to match teacher needs and library resources. This approach requires active observation and listening. Needs may be curriculum-based or personal, intellectual or social. Teachers may need to develop a summer reading list: *voila*—the librarian's suggestions! They may need a good novel for escape: *voici*—the best-seller or comfy golden oldie! What to do with students who whiz through the material? Have them create HyperCard stacks in the library as tutorials for slower-achievers.

Librarians should also recognize and take advantage of the formal and informal groups that the exist within the school. Do certain teachers "hang around" together? Are certain departments close knit? In helping one teacher, the librarian may attract a whole set of teachers as word gets around. One might become Machiavellian in approach; however, being conscious of natural social and professional links is smart thinking. Librarians can graciously make use of these networks to gain greater access to teachers, thus providing more service to students. Again, the more that one-to-one interaction occurs based on mutual interest, the more concrete the ensuing partnership. In Section 9, Helen Flowers lists 68 ways to "catch" a teacher; these ideas can inspire librarians to look at the needs around them and "hook" teachers by satisfying their needs.

Note that teachers may not be aware of some needs. For example, after listening to student frustration about learning some difficult concept, the librarian may see that a teacher needs to supplement the textbook. The teacher might not be aware of that need and may feel that more lectures or more homework are needed instead. In such a case, the librarian may proceed in a couple of ways.

First, by responding to the students' voiced needs by showing them useful library resources on their topic, the librarian demonstrates concern.

Second, the librarian may talk with the teachers, making them aware of the students' needs. This approach requires a great amount of trust since it implies a need to change, which is difficult to accept from another person. If librarians start by listening to expressed needs and responding to them, they will probably be well occupied for some time. And they will have done the groundwork necessary to address unexpressed needs.

Meet with teacher groups:

While attracting is a good first step, librarians need to demonstrate that they mean business by meeting with teacher groups professionally. What regular meetings occur? Do subject or level groups discuss issues on a consistent basis? What task forces need library input? By examining the school meeting schedule, librarians can encourage a broader perspective; they can actively participate in school affairs by attending these meetings.

Developing partnerships requires getting out of the library, just as teachers can't use the library effectively behind their desks. Even if each teacher had a computer in the classroom with access to the library's holdings, librarians would need to meet with teachers on their own ground. Inviting groups into the library gives the librarian a chance to promote the library's resources.

While you might want to just sit in on a meeting, it's usually a good idea to have a concrete reason for attending. It's a good opportunity to slant the library's resources and services to that group's particular needs. A librarian with a talent for mathematical recreational games can give a five-to-ten minute mini-lesson about Lewis Carroll's logic puzzles, getting the teachers involved in the process, and follow the talk with a booklist of fun math titles and an offer to give the presentation in their classes. When teachers see that librarians know about their subject area, they may be more receptive to librarian partnerships.

By attending meetings, librarians hear about school problems: how can teachers help an increasingly diverse student population; what are different ways to evaluate student learning; how can students learn about current Latin American literary trends; how should the school approach the AIDS issue? Librarians can offer their services by developing resource lists of in-house materials or local agencies. They can do research on the topic of concern. They can connect teachers with experts in the field. They can work on ad hoc committees as equal partners in educational problem-solving. They can help develop grant proposals to address issues. All these efforts demonstrate to groups of teachers specific ways that librarians and libraries provide significant access to information—and ways to work with that information.

Plan and implement one-time activities:

How do you win a campaign? One voter at a time. That's the basic lesson in winning over teachers and developing successful partnerships. As teachers experience the positive results of effective planning with librarians, they will seek further opportunities to expand those partnerships. Maybe a teacher wants the students to have current information about a scientific development, such as biotechnology. A perfect opportunity for class information instruction exists. The librarian and teacher can plan a period during which students can learn how to use *Infotrac* or other periodical indexes while gathering recent information about biotechnology. The teacher can evaluate how well students tie in their findings to their classwork, and the librarian can evaluate how well students found and evaluated information sources.

Perhaps a teacher wants a way to help students critique their oral delivery. The librarian can supply videotaping equipment and student crew for the class, and can help the teacher plan ways for students to critically view and evaluate speeches.

A teacher covering the Middle Ages may want students to explore different aspects of the times. If, in the past, the librarian worked with students individually, pointing out to each one the many areas where information can be found, he or she might talk with the teacher and suggest that a "pathway" about the Middle Ages be produced, accompanied by a short presentation or scavenger hunt for relevant sources throughout the library. If the resultant reports are more interesting and substantial than before, the teacher will be more open to partnering with the librarian in the future.

Essentially, librarians who want to build partnerships need to look at their own past experiences with adults and students, and think of ways to improve them. They need to listen to concerns and ideas, and respond effectively with feasible ideas for joint solutions. Whether the result is a product, an instructional session, a display or event, improved student outcomes will lead to the next step in partnership-building.

Legitimize Structures
Formalize partnerships:

Once word gets around that the library has good resources and services, it's time to formalize partnerships. The library needs official "blessing" as an active educational partner, particularly from administrators. Specific instructional/curricular roles need to be clarified so the entire school community understands the relationship.

Ideally, teacher-librarian partnerships should not be mandated from above, but rather be the natural result of school-wide awareness and deliberation. If faculty don't "own" the decision, then it will be harder for the librarian to get cooperation.

Establish a library board:

A good way to develop this type of backing is to institute a library board or steering committee. Composed of teacher, administrative, and student representatives, this group can provide valuable insights into the workings of the school and the sometimes unvoiced needs that the library can address. These people act as ears for the librarian, outposts for those areas where a librarian may not frequent. Perhaps students want leisure seating or magazines to cut up; perhaps teachers need a place to store papers or educational publications; perhaps administrators need workshops videotaped or a literature review on independent study programs. Board members can also help solve library problems of theft, noise, or other library abuse by offering different solutions and enforcing subsequent library action. The group offers two-way communication and action between the school and the library—and can form the core of schoolwide library planning.

The advisory board also serves as library advocates, communicating library needs and services to the rest of the school. The group would be aware of a constrained library budget and could let others know of the library's dilemma, adding credance to librarian demands for more funds. The group could help decide on and plan library events, insuring wider participation before and during the program.

In one school, a science fiction "conference" was held in the library. Student "hackers" demonstrated library computer programs to the public, library interns made a maze for younger attendees, the adults found a local science fiction writer who was honored at the event's reception, art teachers publicized a program cover contest, another teen group videotaped the day, and local merchants donated door prizes. As a result, 450 people came on a Saturday to enjoy a most successful event. This kind of participation would not have been possible without a well-established board acting as liaisons and planners.

Join committees:

While some librarians align themselves with a specific department or other school subgroup, those who join schoolwide committees are probably in the best position politically. (In a few cases, librarians become part of an administrative team, but this managerial viewpoint is rare, unfortunately.) For long-term, significant partnerships, librarians should be members of curriculum-development committees. Not only do they get to see what courses and approaches are being considered, but they can help shape the curriculum and develop related resources. If librarians see valuable resources being overlooked, they can suggest course units that could take advantage of existing materials.

The more that librarians can participate as active members of meaningful committees, the more they are regarded by teachers as substantial forces within the school—and as equal partners in education. Librarians would be welcome additions to strategic planning and accreditation committees (two wonderful opportunities to understand a school's governance) as well as alternative instructional programs, such as contract work or independent study committees, in-service and professional development committees and evaluation committees. Committee membership should highlight librarian resourcefulness, cross-discipline expertise, and helpfulness.

Integrate and Expand the System

Once librarians are integrated into both the academic formal and informal systems in a school, they are in a position to offer a full range of library resources and materials to the different constituencies. They can effectively make the systems work for them—to serve the school community.

Develop a range of library services:

Early on, a librarian might have to proceed cautiously, focusing effort on listening closely to the expressed needs of the school community. While that active listening must continue, eventually the librarian can become more active on a broader plane. A strong mission statement about the library's goals can be constructed, with help from the library board. Based on that guiding principle, the librarian can then develop a range of objectives about resources and services, which can be prioritized depending on school factors (e.g., curriculum, staffing, finances, student characteristics).

Note that goals imply planning for the future. A first list of services would probably include those services that can be provided at present, using existing resources. The list might include ongoing services or might expand present offerings that need no additional material support. A more far-reaching list of services would include those items that cannot be supplied now, but could benefit the school if more resources were available. The first list says, in effect, "Here's what the library can do for you *now*." The second asserts, "Given sufficient resources and support, the library could *really* help you by offering ..."

Here are some sample library services that can be improved with librarian-teacher planning:

☐ An essential service is instruction to insure that students become information literate. They need to be able to locate, evaluate, interpret, organize, and share information. Indeed, current educational literature emphasizes the need to teach these critical thinking skills more—and teach fewer specific facts. Librarians and teachers can work together to develop:

- articulated literacy skills instruction throughout the curricula so concepts can be introduced and mastered in terms of subject areas.
- research courses on the use of specialized reference sources so students can develop different research strategies and locate specialized reference tools;
- half-hour resource "interviews" with all students doing research papers so the librarian can review their strategies and suggest added sources to consider;
- peer instruction on use of CD-ROM products.

☐ Both teachers and librarians should encourage reading. Several means to motivate students include:

- bibliography bookmarks that list exciting books grouped by reading level or subject;
- storytelling workshops and peer storytelling so older students can read to eager younger students;
- holiday gift book ideas so parents can reinforce good reading habits at home;

☐ Programs and events provide enrichment learning opportunities. Several approaches may be used:

- activities for national library-related weeks such as Children's Book Week, National Library Week, Banned Books Week;
- curriculum-related events such as a Renaissance Fair or a women's seminar;
- computer and other courses for parents offered in the evening.

☐ Librarians and teachers can produce displays to provide dramatic, visual stimuli. These presentations take the form of:

- exhibits of student work, both of art and of reports;
- tie-ins with educational broadcasting;
- community exhibits and fairs that show students outside resources and opportunities;
- reading promotion displays that complement classroom literature.

☐ Librarians and teachers can produce documents that help the entire school community:

- library newsletters to inform faculty, parents, and friends about library activities and needs;
- research guides;

- bibliographies to provide curriculum support and advice for leisure-time readers;
- slide-tape library orientations.

☐ Libraries can also serve as the forum for original work and production:
- student books and reports that reveal their feelings;
- student HyperCard stacks collections;
- teacher transparencies collection.

☐ To provide effective service, it is necessary to develop a strong collection. This task includes several aspects:
- acquisition of curriculum-related materials;
- expansion of professional collections;
- development of the multicultural collection including materials for ESL (English as a second language) students;
- networking with area schools to provide resource-sharing;
- targeted withdrawal of materials to offer the most accurate and up-to-date information.

☐ Teachers and librarians can work together on fund-raising on several fronts:
- library participation in school fund-raisers to show school support;
- adopt-a-book programs;
- the sale of customized stationery and other computer-generated products using library computers;
- writing grant proposals with curriculum departments to acquire resources.

In developing a range of services, librarians can offer a menu of possibilities from which teachers can choose. In terms of potential services, the board and the librarian can create different scenarios and prioritizations, and work with the rest of the school to implement the most useful possibilities.

Target a group of teachers:

While a range of services may be developed, a scattershot approach to library service in which a librarian tries to be all things to all people, usually does not work well. The library and librarian get better mileage if either a horizontal or vertical partnership is used. For example, a library may do one task well for all partners, such as creating "pathway" bibliographies or developing exciting storytelling times at all levels or planning a variety of tasks with one targeted group, such as the sixth grade teachers or the science department. Either perspective may "classify" the librarian (as a good storyteller or as a science expert), but at least high-quality, focused service will result in professional partnership credibility. Then the librarian can transfer the resources and services to parallel groups.

Targeting a group for in-depth partnership has the advantage of showing off a variety of library services. If, for instance, you focus on the science department, you need to look at the library collection in terms of the science curriculum, to keep up with scientific developments, and to be a science advocate. Some general guidelines for working with any target population follow include:

- Be familiar with the curriculum and associated trends.
- Attend related faculty planning and organizational meetings.
- Discover faculty needs for curriculum and professional development.
- Provide tangible library service geared to the curriculum: bibliography, display, lesson, pathway, literature review.
- Plan an extensive unit in collaboration with faculty.
- Plan and implement curriculum-related events or programs such as guest authors, films, or library-subject scavenger hunts.
- Use faculty input to improve library holdings in each subject area.
- Help faculty develop their own resources and resource-sharing.
- Help plan and implement future curricular direction.
- Promote the department's work with the library throughout the school.

Provide in-service workshops:

One aspect of partnership planning that is sometimes overlooked is faculty training. Teachers may recognize a problem or need but not know how to solve it. Librarians can use this situation to their advantage to provide service.

Professional development occurs daily in a learning community. As teachers and librarians work together, they share their knowledge and each one benefits. "Training" can consist of a fruitful discussion during lunch about good historical fiction to use for a Civil War unit or about effective criteria for evaluating computer software. Training can also consist of a one-hour tutorial on how to use the latest laserdisc product.

While these spontaneous individual sessions are useful in reinforcing partnerships, formal training for teacher groups is also needed. Each school has its own method of providing such in-service training, and librarians should make use of the structure that is in place.

Who plans training? How are training topics determined? What is the training calendar, and how far in advance is it set? Who does the training? When librarians know the answers to these questions, they are in a better position to insure that teachers learn the necessary skills to help students make best use of the library and its resources.

Librarians can either find others to train teachers, or they can conduct training themselves. One advantage of library networking is that librarians can call upon each other to train their respective staffs. Such outside expertise can complement in-house skill and increase teacher respect for librarianship.

Regardless of the trainer, the librarian needs to help determine the content of the workshop. What will be covered? What is the time frame? How will participants practice new skills? How will learning be integrated into teacher classroom use? The librarian should determine:

- what presentation methods are most effective: demonstration, audio-visual, small group work, etc.;
- how groups should be arranged in order to insure social reinforcemnts though opportunities for group discussion and practice;
- what kind of evaluation best reflect participants' prior experience and learning.

In Section 9 Augie E. Beasley and Carolyn G. Palmer provide helpful hints in conducting teacher workshops. They also offer a variety of topics for possible in-services. By studying these examples, librarians can prepare training that enables teachers to teach more effectively—and plan more extensively and knowledgably with librarians.

Establish a school-wide partnership plan:

Once as teachers, individually and in small groups, and librarians establish strong partnerships, the way has been paved for school-wide planning. It is at this point that a cross-curricular and cross-grade information-literacy curriculum can be developed and implemented. Such a curriculum should include information access (including information in other settings); critical evaluation (including content analysis); interpretation (including visual skills); organizing (including such tools as HyperCard); and sharing (including dramatizations and debates). Once a school-wide partnership begins to form, long-range resource development and maintenance can be integrated fully into the school's mission. At this point, librarians can help form the school's vision for effective student learning.

Teacher Survey

By participating in this survey, you will help us discover how we can better serve you and your students. Thank you for your time.

1. In which of the following ways do your students use the library? (Circle all that apply.)

Class as a whole   Small groups   Individuals

2. Which of the following kinds of assignments requiring the use of the library do you give? (Circle all that apply.)

Oral reports   Debate assignments   Research papers
Book reports   Reading biographies   Reading fiction
Other:

3. How would you rate the library has a help to you in teaching?

Essential   Important   Useful   Not useful

4. The librarian is helpful in making suggestions about new materials that might be useful to your students.

Strongly agree   Agree   Disagree   Strongly disagree

5. The librarian is helpful in acquiring new materials for your students.

Strongly agree   Agree   Disagree   Strongly disagree

6. The librarian is helpful in assisting your students with their library work.

Strongly agree   Agree   Disagree   Strongly disagree

7. The library has an adequate collection in your subject area.

Strongly agree   Agree   Disagree   Strongly disagree

8. The library orientation class is helpful.

Strongly agree   Agree   Disagree   Strongly disagree

9. The library is useful for your own research or pleasure reading.

Strongly agree   Agree   Disagree   Strongly disagree

10. Please complete the following sentences:

One of the greatest strengths of our library program is:

One part of the library program that needs improvement is:

Please make any additional comments on the back of this sheet.

Adapted from a survey used by Brenda Brown, Librarian at the Branson School, Ross, California

Section 3

The Planning Process

Along each step in partnership development, some basic questions need to be answered by the librarian and teacher who are planning together.

☐ The partners must define the audience: students, teachers, parents, community.
- What are their needs in terms of information?
- What background do they have that can help shape learning?
- What do they need to know ahead of time, or what do they need to prepare ahead of time?

☐ The partners must clarify the objective:
- Do they hope to facilitate student learning, faculty education, public relations, fund-raising?
- What changes in behaviors or attitudes are desired? How will they be measured?

☐ The partners must negotiate the content:
- What information or library skills will be addressed?
- What aspects of the subject area will be covered?

☐ The partners must determine what resources will be used:
- Will resources come from the library, from the classroom, from students, from outside resources?
- Who will supply them: the librarian, the teacher, students, other agencies, other persons?
- How available are they? Do students need to look off-site, or will the librarian or teacher get the resources for the learners?

☐ The partners must determine the delivery system:
- Lecture, videotape, learning packet, a combination of formats?
- Do supporting materials exist, or do they have to be produced? Who will create the original materials?

☐ The partners must determine the time frame:
- Is this a one-time project? If so, when should it be scheduled? Can it be tied into other school activities?
- Will it need to be divided into smaller time periods? If so, will classes be arranged weekly or daily?
- What follow-up time is needed?

☐ The partners need to decide in what location the activity will be most effective:

- How do the presence of other people, of resource materials, of the facility's nature itself (i.e., furniture, space, accessibility), as well as the movement patterns of the participants (i.e., where are they coming from and where are they going after the activity) affect the decision?
- Should a combination of locations be used? In some cases, different portions of the activity, such as a slide-tape presentation or student practice, may take occur at different sites.
- How available is the space? Are other people using it?
- What seating or other furniture is needed? Does the area need to be re-arranged?
- Is transportation a factor? If the activity is off-site, someone has to arrange and pay for transportation. What kind of transportation will be used? Who will drive? How is everyone covered in terms of insurance? Who will take care of details?

☐ The partners must decide who will teach or present the information.

- How will instructional duties be determined: by interest, capability, availability?
- Will more than one person be involved?
- Will off-site people be used? Are their needs (e.g., transportation, fees, equipment) met?

☐ The partners must design the learning activity:

- When and where will student practice occur?
- Will students work independently or in groups?
- Will homework be assigned?
- What standards of performance and supervision will be required?

☐ Finally, the partners must plan how the activity will be evaluated:

- What will be evaluated: the plan, the delivery/activity itself, the results?
- Who will be evaluated: the students, other participants, the teacher, the librarian?
- What evaluation tools will be used: observation, response sheets, tests, product evaluation?
- Who will evaluate: the students, observers, the teacher, the librarian, a supervisor?
- How will evaluation results be used: to grade students, to improve the planning process, to improve partnerships?

- Partners should be aware that, in general, more than one constituent should evaluate, and more than one evaluation tool should be used.

Whether the planning results in a lesson, a contest, a document, or a fund-raiser, these questions provide a framework for useful discussion—and implementation. As partnerships develop, thorough planning marks successful encounters and facilitates further growth.

<u>Notes</u>

Section 4
Information Literacy

What is the business of the school library? The information business (its acquisition and organization) *and* the education business (teaching others how to access and use information). Librarian-teacher partnerships will probably focus on helping students become information literate, but it should be noted that information can be used for personal reasons and it can be fun.

The strongest basis for planning is a well-defined, information literacy curriculum developed and accepted by the entire school and incorporated throughout the curriculum. Several good guides exist. Most include the following competencies for students:

- location: of sources, and of information within a source;
- evaluation: of sources, and of information within a source;
- interpretion of information;
- organization of information;
- sharing of information.

When lessons are developed, care should be taken to include:

- print and non-print sources;
- visual, aural, as well as written literacy;
- instruction on care and use of equipment;
- encouragement of reading as a life-long, enjoyable activity;
- multicultural experiences;
- multi-sensory opportunities for learning.

As librarians, in partnership with teachers, examine each concept or skill, they need to make several decision:

- At what point in the student's development should each competency be introduced, mastered, and reinforced or reviewed? Grade level might not be the best determinant; prior experiences of students and "readiness" vary greatly even within the same age group. Ideally, individualized or small group lesson plans let students learn at their own pace.
- In what subject areas should be competency be "couched"? Perhaps one subject or learning unit is particularly appropriate for presenting

a concept. In other cases, a skill may be introduced in a variety of disciplines, permitting reinforcement of the competency.

- What roles do librarians and teachers play in teaching each competency? As the planning process and partnerships improve, this issue becomes easier to determine.

In implementing a curriculum, librarians usually find that certain individual teachers or groups of teachers will be the most active partners. The basis for such strength may be a natural affinity for libraries or it may be founded upon interpersonal connections, such as similar academic training or personalities. For example, the librarian who feels comfortable with computers might develop a good partnership with teachers who are interested in technology. The more educationally sound the foundation, the more likely that the partnership will blossom.

Librarians can approach information literacy instruction via department or grade level or the scope can be interdepartmental and intergrade. A typical approach might involve presentation of general reference tools, followed by specific strategies organized by topic. Alternatively, librarians may pose "trivia" questions at the beginning of a unit to expose students to specialized references. After instruction, the librarian can provide guidance on materials as students need them. A third alternative might focus on a subject's application to the real world. Using mathematics as an example, librarians might pose questions about cooking or economics in consumer activities, which can be answered by using library references.

Here is a suggested sequence for covering information literacy competencies. As with all aspects of the educational program, it can become richer through partner planning.

Primary Grades

Location:
- Finding your way through a book.
- Finding pictures of families in picture books.
- Alphabet soup: finding books by author.

Evaluation:
- Is this book too hard for me?
- How to tell a book by its cover.

Interpretation:
- What do pictures tell us?
- What fits in this story, what doesn't?
- Dancing to poetry rhythm.

Organization:

- Classifying fairytales: by character, mood, country, etc.
- Drawing pictures of different aspects of stories.

Sharing:

- Acting out stories.
- Making character puppets.
- Creating a radio show from sources.
- Playing a game based on a story.

Equipment use:

- Audiocassettes.
- VCRs.

Reading encouragement:

- Puppet reinactment of stories.
- Booktalks from student-made posters.

Upper Elementary

Location:

- Creating catalog cards for original student work.
- Mapping encyclopedia cross-references.
- Developing word trees using the dictionary.

Evaluation:

- Comparing dictionaries and encyclopedias.
- Comparing two biographical sources.
- Comparing fiction and nonfiction treatments of history.

Interpretation:

- Writing other endings to stories.
- Creating original folktales.
- Tracing changing boundaries over time.

Organization:

- Creating graphs.
- Making book bingo cards.
- Making simple time lines.

Sharing:

- Making collages of stories.
- Dressing up as an historical or literary character.
- Creating dioramas from stories.

Equipment use:

- Cameras.
- Transparencies.

Reading encouragement:

- Creating games from stories.
- Using BookWhiz database.
- Reading-based contests.

Middle School

Location:

- Using magazine indexes for class speeches.
- Interviewing people.
- Conducting energy surveys.

Evaluation:

- Comparing two magazine articles about a current issue.
- Comparing atlases and globes.
- Comparing men's and women's sports rules.

Interpretation:

- Extrapolating social values from folktales.
- Identifying plants using nature guides.
- Tracing a day via the newspaper.

Organization:

- Mapping information.
- Sequencing developments.
- Creating a visual dictionary

Sharing:

- Producing student bulletin boards.
- Creating comic books on topics.
- Building scale models.

Equipment use:

- Videotaping equipment.
- Computer utility programs.

Reading encouragement:

- Student storytellers.
- Student reviewers.

High School

Location:

- Using poetry indexes to locate poems by subject.
- Using on-line Boolean searching to find subject matter.
- Using almanacs to find economic trends.
- Locating laws about student rights.

Evaluation:

- Comparing primary and secondary sources.

- Examining magazine advertisements for social messages.
- Analyzing propaganda posters.
- Comparing different types of maps.

Interpretation:

- Extrapolating science from science fiction.
- Analyzing career representations in fiction and nonfiction.
- Interpreting psychological problems using different schools of psychology.
- Studying history from the Native American perspective.

Organizing:

- Creating databases.
- Developing HyperCard stacks.
- Tracing animals from Kingdom to genus.
- Writing directions.

Sharing:

- Debating issues.
- Creating mock interviews of historic figures.
- Producing slide-tape programs.
- Developing a heritage hike.

Equipment use:

- Advanced computer applications.
- Telecommunications.

Reading encouragement:

- Student tutors and readers.
- Student-managed magazine.
- Student writing.

Librarians should have an overall perspective of the school's curriculum so they can encourage cross-discipline and cross-age instruction. One effective way to structure such instruction is to use a thematic approach. One school chose "rain forests" as a unifying theme. A core collection of materials floated from classroom to classroom, with instructions for use. The librarian worked with teachers, planning age-appropriate lessons. The results of the students' inquiries and research were displayed in the classrooms and then shared at the school's open house. Parents were impressed with the murals, quizzes, and taped presentations made by the students. Other themes that lend themselves to schoolwide partnerships include historical periods, human subgroups, planets, the arts, seasons and holidays, sports, living things, literary forms.

As teachers and librarians realize the extensive role of information processing skills throughout the curriculum, they can plan significant activities that will help students become lifelong learners.

<u>Notes</u>

Section 5
Programs and Services

A weaving loom displaying arts and crafts books, a poetry read-in, a collection of student-created literary magazines: these exemplify exciting uses of library materials through library programs and other services. Librarians develop events, displays, and documents to educate the school community, often in response to curriculum and other school issues. However, such efforts carry greater weight when done in full partnership with teachers.

Programs

Programs can be effective attention getters; they glamorize the library, making it even more inviting to students and teachers. Relevant topics are more important than expensive, time-consuming productions. Creativity carries more weight than cash. By partnering with teachers, librarians can make the best use of resources—and support. They can share the responsibility of getting the program itself, arranging for its presentation, publicizing it, and participating in it.

Library events, including those that the library co-sponsors with teachers, require thorough planning. A time-table framework provides a simple way to organize these events:

- Four months ahead: decide on a topic and research possible sources of information to present it.
- Three months ahead: develop specific objectives and approaches for the event; there should be a meaningful reason for staging an event so people will be excited about attending. Also compile a specific list of people and suppliers for all aspects of the event including publicity, the presentation, hospitality, transportation as needed, complementary library books.
- Two months ahead: contact potential presenters, giving specifics about the audience, time frame, desired content and outcome.
- One month ahead: check all details of the event including public relations materials, presenter needs, space, handouts, etc.
- Two weeks ahead: distribute public relations material (which should

be prepared a month ahead): press releases, flyers, displays, invitations, TV interviews. Incorporate an event-related contest, such as a program cover competition, to further motivate students.

- One week ahead: map out the event site for activities, equipment, seating, food, etc. Prepare directional signs. Liven up the area, particularly if the event will be staged in the library. Contact event helpers.
- One day ahead: set up the equipment, seating, name tags, registration.
- THE day: get to the site early and deal with last-minute details. Make sure that other people are available to help early-arriving attenders and presenters. Provide beverages and snacks if possible. Have someone take photographs of the event. Have people in charge of gathering evaluation forms and supervising clean-up.
- One day after: evaluate and follow-up. Thank the presenters and all those who helped.

Events are particularly effective if they are the culminating experience of library preparations working in tandem with teacher and community efforts. At Homer Center School in Pennsylvania the faculty wanted to improve student self-esteem and communication skills. Community experts trained faculty and students in collecting family histories. Since the librarians also wanted students to experience storytelling, they arranged for local practitioners to perform at school. Afterwards, students worked on their family trees and wrote folktales. The climatic event was a night of student storytelling of family and traditional tales.

Other successful program ideas include:

- A youth summit on drug abuse and alternative action incorporating community action groups. Having teen speakers provides a bridge between adults and youthful participants. High schoolers can work with the librarian and teachers to develop a summit for middle schoolers.
- Career Week highlights library resources and future possibilities within each curricular area. Teachers and librarians can enlist community speakers for a one-day "conference" format or during class time throughout the week. The library can host career contests, activities, and displays. Career Week is an excellent way to advertise library computer programs about career and college choices. Students can also take aptitude or interest tests in the library, and take the results to the school counselors for guidance, thus tying together two vital services.

- The library can host a teen panel on peer pressure or some other youth issue. Faculty and the librarian can recommend good student speakers and train them in panel discussion techniques. Again, library displays publicize and reinforce the event.

- The library can offer workshops on cartooning or other ways to express information, such as animation or photography. Hands-on experience excites youthful attendees and shows that the library is "with it." The National Endowment for the Humanities provides grants for innovative library programs that enable youth to discuss the profound implications of the humanities. For example, the cartooning session could be incorporated into a session on political cartoons and social commentaries.

- Science magic programs encourage youth to explore scientific activities. Displayed library resources (and bibliographies) provide immediate means to pursue this subject.

- Schools emphasize interdepartmental links when they develop thematic celebrations such as a Medieval Fete, Renaissance Fair, or Earth Day. Participants choose from several activities, such as demonstrations, dances, arts, games, food, sports. The library provides research materials, displays books, and operates a thematic "booth."

- An Arts Festival showcases the efforts or creative students and community members. The library can display works and hold poetry readings, readers' theater, or musical performances.

- A Conservation Event provides an opportunity for the library to work with science classes and social issues clubs to share conservation concerns and solutions through research, displays, and contests.

- As a means to broaden the concept of communication and information, a sign language demonstration attracts attention and affirms human diversity.

- The library expands beyond the four walls in sponsoring a survival seminar. Displays and bibliographies show off applicable library resources.

- A day when students dress as a favorite character encourages reading—and is fun, free publicity.

- An outdoor evening program on astronomy puts the library in a good light, showing how information works day and night. This event can also be combined with evening poetry readings or read-alouds.

- A library-conducted safety demonstration complements associated resources and supports school and community safety efforts.
- Kite-flying demonstrations lift user spirits and give the library an opportunity to profile sports books.

Contests

A contest is a specialized type of event. Since it demands involvement, it has good potential for learning. Contests vary from questions of the week to scavenger hunts, from crossword puzzles to circulation raffles. In each case, good contests should be easy to enter, have easy rules, a sense of suspense and a balance between skill and luck. Most of all, contests must be fun with lots of opportunities for winning.

As with other programs, effective contests are the result of librarian-teacher partnerships. When contests tie into other school and library activities, they have the advantage of shared publicity and support. And, of course, the library is seen as an integral part of the total school community.

When designing contests, teacher-librarian partners should clarify:
- the goal or objective: is the contest to highlight library resources, to raise school consciousness, to improve the library's image;
- the rules: for participation and for winning;
- the time frame: beginning and ending times, total time limit;
- the resources: what supplies are available, what contestants supply or can use;
- the prizes.

Here are some contest ideas with examples that combine library and other aspects of school:
- anagrams of outstanding people, titles, library terms, locations;
- trivia questions about animals, geography, history, literature;
- Encyclopedia Brown and other literary mysteries for contestants to solve;
- crossword puzzles about science, authors, art, sports, technology;
- book cover contests;
- computer program or HyperCard design;
- research scavenger hunts;
- bingo about drug facts, school sights, environment;
- costumes of historical figures, literary characters, science fiction creatures;
- guess the number of books, magazines, pages, videos, CDs;
- finish nursery rhymes, songs, poems, quotations.

In planning contests, librarians can follow these steps:
- Plan a budget far in advance.
- Determine the objective and choose a theme to carry it out.
- Gather contest supplies: buttons, stickers, forms.
- Get prizes donated from business and school associates; consider gifts of time or fines amnesties.
- Calculate contest variations to insure the widest possible participation. For example, create more elusive clues for adults or older students.
- As with other events, publicize widely, arrange and monitor carefully, and thank generously.

Displays

An attractive way to promote information is to display it. Through teacher-librarian partnerships a combination of visuals and text can act as entertaining "stations" where students can self-monitor their learning.

Several issues go into planning displays:
- What is the objective of the display: to promote overlooked books, to raise social consciousness, to show off student efforts?
- What will be displayed: books, pictures, games, realia?
- Where will display items will come from: library, classroom, community?
- What will be the balance between graphics and text?
- What accompanying materials will be included: bibliographies, flyers, bookmarks?
- What connection will the display have with other activities: clubs, curriculum, national observances, school events?
- Who will assemble and take down the exhibit: librarian, teacher, student, outside agency?
- Where will the display be exhibited: library, classroom, school hall, in the community?
- How long will the display continue: a week, a month? (After a while a display loses its novelty and will be overlooked.)

If the librarian uses a simple and dramatic combination of images and text, if the librarian changes the display regularly to sustain a sense of novelty, if the librarian gets teachers and students involved with displays both in planning and in interacting with the display, if the librarian ties the display to the rest of the school, then the display will be effective—and worth the effort.

No matter how good the content and involvement, displays also need to be attractive. In Section 9, Marilyn Fredrickson and Jane Cabaya offer "Design Basics." Displayers should practice looking at commercial displays: in stores, in public places, at conferences. How does the space dimension define the display? What display features attract the viewer? What three-dimensional features make the display "come alive?" Does the display invite interaction? What professional touches are used? Aesthetic techniques are around for the asking—and the using.

Documents

Documents comprise a major library activity. Libraries produce a variety of documents for a variety of reasons: orientation slide shows, instructional videos and audiocassettes, research and topical HyperCard stacks, booklists and pathways, bookmarks, signs, flyers, newsletters, manuals, charts, transparencies, learning packets. In most cases, library documents model the effective results of information literacy: the ability to select, evaluate, interpret, organize, and present information.

As with other areas of programs, document planners need to consider objectives, audience, message, format, resources (time, money, equipment), desired response or action and evaluation. Naturally, all documents need to meet the standards of all library services and programs: appropriateness, clarity, accuracy, attractiveness.

When documents are produced in partnership with teachers, they can more adequately meet the needs of the rest of the school and thus get greater use. In addition, responsibilities for producing documents can be shared between librarians and teachers according to individual expertise. Even if teachers are minimally involved in document production, they can pilot-test and otherwise evaluate the results. In that way, they become more aware of library products, and they can publicize the library documents. Likewise, librarians can provide the research background for teacher-produced documents that make the teacher look good—and be grateful for the behind-the-scenes effort of the librarian.

If teachers approve a library-produced guide sheet on bibliographic form, for example, then students have a useful reference tool—and the librarian has helped coalesce teachers. In counterpoint, in Section 9, Joanne Stewart offers generic guidelines for producing "Infinite Bibliographies," customized and individualized bibliographies. Curriculum- based computer databases are another example of joint planning and implementation.

Original Information

In a way, library documents can be considered as original work, but a separate service that results from teacher-librarian partnership is archives of original works done by the school community. By storing and making available in-house works, the library insures an historical picture of the school as well as providing valuable current information.

Many librarians routinely save school yearbooks, handbooks, and programs. Several keep course syllabi and student publications such as literary magazines and newspapers. However, how many keep student reports, teacher transparencies, and class collages? Think of the many hours that go into creating reports; they can be incorporated into vertical files. Transparencies for stories, for example, can be housed in the library for several teachers to use in literature-based reading programs. Student collages and posters can be the basis for effective library displays. Some grades have book-making projects; a section of the library can hold these special original efforts for young writers to show younger readers in future years.

The basic premises for providing archival service for original in-school work are to recognize and acknowledge student and teacher effort and to expand the usefulness of original work to help the broader school community and its future members.

Computer-Related Service

Computers are becoming an integral part of library service as education enters the 21st century. Computers are also a great partnership tool that can be used on a variety of levels:

- as a tool for students and teachers to use for their independent work (e.g., creating databases, word processing, desktop publishing);
- as a means of curriculum reinforcement (e.g., tutorials, simulations, enrichment courseware);
- as an administrative tool (e.g., creating tests, grading);
- as an access tool to information on CD-ROM, on-line databases, and other telecommunication-transferable information;
- as an authoring tool to combine information media;
- as a means of sharing information through student-produced databases, HyperCard stacks, games and multimedia reports.

Providing computers in the library sends the message that the library is truly an information center. Students can use reference books freely in the library, keeping them accessible on-site, while writing papers. Students transfer class offerings to the library as they use curriculum-based software. Students and teachers have access through modems to the broader world of information; the library is really "connected." In Section 9, Margaret Schmude, for one, celebrates "Online Serendipity."

Librarian-teacher partnerships reinforce computer access and use, and provide a broader-based support system upon which to expand. While computers are recognized as aids for developing "written" reports, their use can be expanded to "repackage" research results. Here are a few examples:

- Imaginary correspondence between famous people;
- Crossword puzzles or anagrams about a research subject;
- Simulated newspapers for a date in history, such as July 4, 1776;
- Brochures about artists or famous sites;
- Computer-generated comics about social concerns;
- Menus in foreign languages;
- Time-lines of achievements or events;
- HyperCard stacks that trace explorations;
- Calendars that highlight famous "firsts."

Teachers can interact anywhere along the computer-related library service planning spectrum: from acquisitions to incorporation into the curriculum, from order requests to issues of copyright, from linkages between programs to networked systems, from training to troubleshooting. Joint planning insures greater, more effective computer use—and expansion of related service.

Section 6

Collection Development

Throughout this book, collaborative planning for effective library service has been the key. However, the assumption has been that partners will work with the existing collection. No collection is static—or should remain so. Just as teaching methods change and students change, so information and the accompanying library collection demand constant change and revision. As with other aspects of the library, teacher-librarian partnerships strengthen collection development.

Acquisitions

Theoretically, librarians should always consult teachers when ordering materials. Since school libraries basically support the school curriculum, school librarians should work closely with faculty to choose appropriate materials—both for classroom collections as well as for the library. Care should also be taken to insure that adequate leisure reading is purchased for students and teachers.

Different schools vary in their policy about where materials will be kept. Sometimes the professional collection is held in the faculty room; sometimes teachers purchase their own videotapes to keep in their classrooms. While librarians may advocate central purchasing and holdings to insure the most cost-effective and broad-based use, as long as thorough *access* can be guaranteed (usually through librarian-driven, accurate inventory maintenance and easy-to-use check out system), the physical location of materials isn't crucial.

Librarians should have selection policies set in place, to be shared with teachers. (It's surprising how few teachers are aware of such library policies!) This kind of professional preparation provides consistent criteria for acquisitions; particularly with today's budgetary constraints, a strong selection policy insures equitable treatment among teacher groups. It also guards against teacher-driven acquisitions that force librarians into a subservient role.

Having teachers evaluate potential purchases for the library using professional criteria, facilitates greater "ownership" in the acquisitions process and encourages greater use in classrooms. Moreover, evaluation and selection criteria for different media can be very helpful for those teachers wishing to purchase items for their own use. Librarians can provide an additional service by keeping media catalogs and periodicals to help teachers locate possible materials.

Since software seems to be difficult for some teachers to assess, librarians can provide valuable evaluation criteria and reviews. Beyond the selection of individual titles, librarians can also make sure that overall software acquisitions are well-coordinated. To make the best use of computer technology, librarians and teachers should work together to develop strong and useable computer software collections. Some points that librarians can share with teachers in this task include:

- selecting materials that attract and interest students;
- purchasing materials based on student and curricular needs;
- choosing materials that operate similarly and use the same "protocols" as those already in the collection;
- acquiring reputable software that includes regular up-grade options;
- buying generic or utility programs that can be adapted to different subject areas;
- including remedial programs to reinforce basic skills;
- investing in software that reflects current trends;
- insuring that software furthers an overall balance in the collection.

Timing is crucial, and affects acquisitions. When new courses are being developed, the librarian needs to know so the library can support the change with library collection offerings in time for the opening classes. If a teacher has a sudden, significant need for a specific resource, the librarian should try to fulfill that need. Note that a permanent acquisition may not be feasible or advisable for such requests; rather than expecting the library to house all needed information, one anticipates that the library can *access* needed information.

As librarians and teachers help each other locate and acquire needed materials for the school, they support each other's efforts and help coordinate school-wide collection development. One good practice is to channel all purchase orders through the librarian to check for possible duplication and the most cost-effective suppliers. Another habit is to publicize all new acquisitions, sharing these materials at faculty meetings. The more that all teachers and librarians know what is being acquired, the more those items can be used widely.

Professional Collections

An often neglected part of collection development, and a natural for partnerships, is professional reading. Typically, teachers and administrators buy references for their own use, keeping them at home or in their classroom or desk area. While some materials apply strictly to one teacher's work, more often those items would benefit several faculty members. The library is a logical, cost-effective center for those resources.

Representative types of materials include:

- subject-based books and periodicals;
- age-based books and periodicals;
- teaching/learning theory and practice materials;
- AV equipment, manuals and tutorials;
- teaching aids such as transparencies, slides, bulletin board materials, worksheets, models, in-house produced materials;
- administrative/course management resources such as test-making or puzzle-generating software.

Ideally, the professional collection should be the result of school-wide coordinated planning. Teachers and librarians should look at student outcomes and teaching behaviors, and then select those resources that are most cost-effective. Librarians then purchase, process, publicize, and circulate those items. Because professional association dues and subscriptions are usually assigned to a different budget, teachers could bring their journals to the library as soon as they peruse them so other faculty can read them as well.

In actuality, librarians usually have to approach professional collection development teacher by teacher. As a few faculty members donate their magazine issues, the librarian lets the rest of the faculty know that these materials are now available for everyone's use. Similarly, if a teacher requests a professional title, the librarian should acquire it quickly (if it's a good-quality product) and circulate it widely. In addition, as with other requested materials, if all orders go through the librarian, costs can be held down and unnecessary duplications can be eliminated. Successful efforts to develop and use professional materials lead to increased faculty acceptance of and involvement in this valuable collection.

Resource-Sharing

The library is becoming known as an "access to information" center more than an information warehouse. Therefore, neither students nor teachers should expect to find all needed resources "in-house." Rather than decry the library's collection limitations, the school community should value the librarian's professional ability to locate and make available resources beyond the school's boundaries. With partnerships, librarians and teachers can pool their networking capabilities in order to maximize resource-sharing.

Librarians and teachers can use various strategies to take advantage of resource-sharing. Librarians can use interlibrary loan procedures to get materials from outside sources, and they usually network with other librarians and know their collections, so they can get materials quickly by calling the appropriate librarian. Whole sections, such as Shakespeare, may be borrowed from another library for class use during a short-term unit. If teachers or librarians attend universities for continuing education courses, they can search university libraries for requested items (channeled through the library), borrow them, and then have the library circulate and collect them.

Librarians or teachers may have access to telecommunications and can search on-line databases or place a request on an electronic bulletin board for information. Sometimes one partner has the equipment, and the other has information about telecommunication services; together they can maximize the value of this electronic access tool.

Circulation

Borrowing policies should facilitate school use of library materials. Having teacher input in developing these policies can result in more realistic use of materials and improved compliance of set policies. A number of circulation issues bear serious consideration by teacher-librarian partners.

- Who should have borrowing rights: students, faculty, parents, community?
- Should the length of circulation depend on user status; i.e., student, teacher?
- Should the length of circulation depend on the medium: magazine, book, CDs, software?
- What should be the length of circulation for reference materials?
- What should be the circulation policies for class sets of materials: time frame, location of use, overdues policy?
- Should circulation policies be modified for class use of materials during a course unit?
- What should be the circulation policies for "floating" collections, particularly between schools?
- What policies should govern the use of reserve materials?
- What should be the circulation policies for materials loaned from other institutions?
- What policies exist on duplicating information? What costs should be included? What copyright issues are involved?

A critical issue in circulation is censorship. Particularly in school libraries, this problem exists because parents expect to control their children's reading in a school environment. There is a sense that all materials in the library should be top-notch, completely advocated by the librarian. While some controversial titles are sidestepped because of limited budgets, selection should not be a whitewashed censoring procedure. Rather, a strong selection policy and equally strong policy on challenged materials should support library decisions.

Having strong teacher-librarian partnerships prepares the library for censorship challenges. In Section 9, Edna Boardman writes extensive "Notes on a Censorship Battle," which succeeded because of school support. Again, when teachers join in the acquisition process, they can answer challenges to materials more knowledgeably.

Withdrawals

Just as important as acquisitions are withdrawals. Librarians must insure accurate and attractive collections. Parallel to a selection policy, a withdrawal or "de-selection" policy guides the process professionally. And parallel to teacher-librarian partnership in purchases is partnership in weeding.

Teachers should be encouraged to tell librarians about outdated, now inaccurate materials. (Science and geography are good candidates for constant vigilance.) It should be noted that sometimes older interpretations can be of interest; historical perspectives, for example, change over time. Librarians and teachers should work together to determine whether to keep these older materials; they can be valuable for longitudinal studies, but may be misleading if no guidance is given students to analyze them critically. Are all parties willing to insure such intellectual intervention, or should all materials be regarded as self-supporting? The decision tests the strength and value of teacher-librarian partnerships.

On a more mundane level, if teachers see ripped or worn out items they can place a note with them so librarians can spot them quickly; this practice is particularly useful when teachers can spot such conditions in classrooms. Teachers may also know about newer editions or better titles to replace older ones. When teachers and librarians inform each other about informational trends and critically review existing materials to make sure they reflect these changes, the resulting collection will better serve the school community.

<u>Notes</u>

Section 7

Fund Raising

Do you have a million-dollar imagination and a hundred dollar budget? Are you frustrated, knowing what could be done but realizing how little can be accomplished with the financial support available? Are your partnerships resulting in higher expectations without the money to realize those demands? One of the major benefits of librarian-teacher partnerships is fund-raising. Each partner gets added support for money, and can help request and justify it.

Librarians should not shy away from communicating, even advertising, their financial constraints. The more teachers and students become aware of library funding, the more supportive they can be. Even when a high periodicals bill is questioned, once people realize the cost of, say, newspaper subscriptions they can see how quickly the funds can be spent. As long as purchases are well justified, there is nothing to hide and everything to communicate.

Here are some steps that will make your budget public relations campaign more effective:

☐ Emphasize library accomplishments achieved at the existing budget level; communicate what additional and improved services are possible with greater funding.

☐ Perform one cost-related service well rather than several services poorly, so that high-quality work can be demonstrated.

☐ Plan ahead. Make the most of available money in terms of library goals.

☐ Submit requests even if no money exists; this action shows administrators what needs are not capable of being met at the present financial support level.

☐ Help other departments make wise and cost-effective purchases.

☐ Make library needs known, formally and informally.

☐ Submit the budget request well before financial decisions are made.

☐ In the budget proposal, note specific items that satisfy the most important library priorities.

☐ Publicize any purchases made, and highlight their use.

Let's say that everyone agrees that the library, and other parts of the school, should be funded more, what can teacher-librarian partnerships accomplish? They can:
- communicate the school's situation;
- identify sources of funding;
- garner support for the library;
- plan fund-raisers;
- write grants for funding;
- ask people (students, parents, alumnae, community) for donations;
- demand that the school place a higher priority on library funding.

Planning Fund-Raisers

Fund-raising is usually most effective when the librarian specifies one or two priority goals. If the goals parallel a grade level or subject area objective, teachers associated with that goal are more likely to enter into a partnership with the librarian. For instance, mathematics teachers and librarians have successfully joined efforts through grant writing to get money for computers, courseware, enrichment books, staffing, workshops, and facilities renovations.

As with other projects, careful planning is necessary. Partners need to insure that:
- sufficient school support exists;
- adequate resources are available;
- enough people can help throughout the fund-raiser;
- "ownership" and participation is broad-based;
- timing is well-calculated to maximize participating and results;
- publicity is wide-spread and well-targeted;
- follow-up and evaluation are thorough;
- the effort is worthwhile and fun!

Sources of Funding

The best sources of funding continues to be individuals, so the best policy is to develop good relations with all who frequent the library or are influenced by it. As people experience pleasant and successful interaction in the library, they are more apt to support it. Notwithstanding, though, partners should explore all available funding sources to help both parties. Here are some places to start:
- Within the school, several constituent groups are possible donors: students, faculty, families, graduates, friends.
- Within the community, neighbors, local businesses, other libraries, and service and social organizations can donate time, money, and gifts-in-kind.

- Professional organizations, both in the library field and in the broader educational arena offer grants and awards for innovative programs and research. They are particularly interested in pilot and cooperative efforts.
- Government funding exists on local, regional, state, and federal levels. Special projects are announced occasionally, so partners need to keep current.
- Private foundations and companies typically support projects that match their own interests. Usually schools have a better chance with local grantors than national ones.

Fund-Raising Ideas

While bake sales can make money for libraries, it makes more sense to make use of existing library resources and services in fund-raising. Libraries should take advantage of their unique status. Librarians should also help their school partners raise money to demonstrate equitable mutual support. They may also develop joint fund-raisers that help both parties. Regardless of the group that will benefit, fund-raising partners should think in terms of low-effort, high-returns money-making projects.

Based on those assumptions, some school-based fund-raising ideas follow.

☐ Product sales should reinforce the library's or school's image: literate, professional, fun:
- Information-based items including books (news and used), non-print items, posters, bookmarks, calendars, magnets from magazine or catalog pictures;
- Computer-customized products such as birthday cards, stationery;
- PR items such as T-shirts and bags;
- Book donation programs for birthdays, graduations, "adoption."

☐ Services make use of partners' expertise and provide positive public relations:
- Tutoring by adults or students;
- Night or continuing school courses: storytelling, computers, research skills;
- Workshops for parents on choosing books, family reading, study skills;
- Book selection service;
- Computer dating service;
- Videotaping of school events and duplication of the tapes;
- Commissions from artists exhibiting in library;
- Outside group use of facilities or equipment.

☐ Events that reinforce library and school resources can be fun, educational, and profitable:
- special presentations and workshops with guest speakers;
- computer, film, video festivals;
- auctions.

Joint fund-raising efforts can cross department and grade level boundaries. Here are some idea-starters:
- Primary grade teachers and librarians hold costume contests with entrance fees and fun prizes.
- Intermediate grade teachers and librarians hold readathons.
- Middle school teachers and librarians produce creative T-shirts to sell.
- High school teachers and librarians develop an arts festival or Renaissance Fair.
- Art students and teachers design calendars; librarians can contribute famous dates in art to make the calendar distinctive.
- Computer students and teachers conduct computer workshops in cooperation with librarians.
- Domestic science teachers and librarians write grants for equipment and supporting books (to be housed in the library, of course).
- English teachers and librarians produce writing guides.
- Foreign language tapes are created in-house, duplicated by the librarian, and sold.
- Health and physical education teachers design wellness programs that are funded by the government and include funding for library books on the topic.
- Mathematics students and teachers tutor in the library.
- School music performances are videotaped by library aides, and duplicated to sell.
- Psychology department seminars on parenting are held in the library.
- Science teachers get research grant money, and include money for information books to be housed in the library.
- Social studies teachers and librarians hold public political forums.
- Vocational guidance teachers and librarians hold career fairs.

Section 8
Evaluation of Partnerships

Effective librarian-teacher partnership requires consistent formative and summative evaluation: How are we doing? How did we do? What can be done better? Not only does evaluation improve partnership relationships and library service, but also it shows the way for new directions in library action. The emphasis should be on maintaining a critical mindset rather than developing sheaves of evaluation forms.

Evaluation is a blanket word that needs to broken down into several aspects. Librarians must be concerned about evaluation of:

- the activity or service;
- the results or effect of the activity or service;
- the planning process;
- the underlying partnership;
- the partners themselves.

In each case, the partners must address the following issues:

- what points will be evaluated;
- how will they be evaluated;
- who will evaluate;
- when and where will evaluation take place;
- who will interpret the findings;
- how will the evaluation results be used.

Library literature and other educational literature deal effectively with evaluation of student progress and professional development. Several guidelines exist for evaluating programs and services. One practice—using small focus groups representing different constituents to plan and evaluate facilitators—makes good use of librarian-teacher partnerships.

Ways to evaluate teacher-librarian partnerships themselves are considered less frequently. Here are some pointers to look for:

☐ Participation:
- How many partnerships have been developed?
- Do a majority of partners meet regularly?
- How long-standing are these partnerships?
- How substantial are the partnerships?

- Is there a sense of "our" library?
- Are teachers there when librarians need them?

☐ Planning:
- What kinds of decisions are made by partners?
- Do partners equitably share the responsibility of planning?
- Are the partners dependable and thorough?
- Is planning done effectively and productively?
- Do plans accurately reflect school needs?
- What is the quality of any resulting plan?

☐ Interpersonal relationships:
- Do partners respect and trust each other?
- Are partners able to accept and negotiate differences?
- Do partners support each other—and their plans?

☐ Results:
- What affect did the activity or product have?
- What helped and what hindered positive results?
- What should be changed and what should be continued?
- How did the results affect the partnership?

Evaluation should look at both the objective and subjective factors in teacher-librarian partnerships. Personal affinities and conflicts need to be acknowledged and dealt with. The issue of being a "nice person" but a "lousy planner" needs to be reconciled. Sometimes tasks can be successfully planned and implemented with little personal agreement. Likewise, great friendships may exist between librarian and teacher with no overlap to effective planning. All kinds of partnerships are viable and should be recognized and nurtured. All can benefit the library and, ultimately and most importantly, the students.

Because teacher-librarian partnerships are so complicated, a better way to look at the total effort is to use portfolio reviews. Basically, an evaluation portfolio is a collection of documents that shows the partners' plans, efforts, progress, and achievements. For partners, a typical portfolio would include surveys, lesson plans, in-house publications, photographs of events and displays, copies of library-aided student research papers, and user statistics. These documents can be sorted and analyzed from several standpoints, depending on the goal of the evaluation.

For all evaluations, the most important steps are to analyze the evaluation and to act upon the findings. What patterns emerge from the data—why? What difference do the results make? Can anything be done? Evaluation is most effective if it facilitates needed change. Partners can get at the underlying problem and can offer feasible solutions.

When implementing solutions, which usually means changing some factor, partners should consider:

☐ Time frame of the problem—and solution:
- Are short-term results sufficient?
- Is the problem a matter of retiring personnel?
- Can the solution wait or is immediate action required?

☐ People involved:
- Can the problem be solved by library personnel?
- Who needs to change?
- Who needs to decide about change?

☐ Perception:
- Is the library the problem, and does it need to change?
- Are people unaware of the library's services, and do they need to be educated?
- Are underlying structures obstacles to good library service, and do they need to be changed?

Regardless of the results, the evaluation needs to be communicated to the school community at large. Suggestions should be acted upon immediately, at least at a token level, if only for image-building. Those who helped with the evaluation need to know that their input makes a difference; even the smallest, tangible change will demonstrate that the people in power listened and responded. This kind of consideration will build more partnerships than a myriad of newsletters or smiles.

<u>Notes</u>

Section 9

Readings

35 Good Reasons to Send a Student to the Library
By Dian Zillner

To promote better use of the library as a place for educational enrichment, the following suggestions could be distributed to the teachers.

> *MEMO:*
> *From the Library*
> *To the Faculty*
> *If you have students who are finished with their class work and you need an additional activity for them, please look over the following list. Let me know if I can help them in any way.*

- ☐ Write an evaluation of a magazine article in your subject field.
- ☐ Preview audiovisual material you can consider for use in class.
- ☐ If we have more than one item on the subject, let the student look at several and then decide which one would work best for your class.
- ☐ Look through the audiovisuals and make a list of items you could use in your class.
- ☐ Use our "cut up" magazines to find materials for a bulletin board.
- ☐ Do research for a report for extra credit, perhaps on a famous person in your field.
- ☐ Research questions to be used with a game board in your subject field.
- ☐ Learn to operate the next machine you plan to use in class. (Then let the student show the audiovisual material in class.)
- ☐ Use the opaque projector to enlarge a drawing for use as a pattern for a project in art or for use on a bulletin board.
- ☐ Use the opaque projector to make a map to use in the classroom.
- ☐ The other students can then fill in the items you want to highlight (where certain authors lived, location of the 13 colonies, etc.).
- ☐ Use quotation books to find an appropriate quotation to title a bulletin board.
- ☐ Find material (books, magazine articles) that can be used by other students in your class.
- ☐ Check on library materials on a specific subject to see if enough information is available to bring the whole class to the library to work on a project.

☐ Come to the library to learn to change a bulb on an audiovisual machine that you use frequently so he or she can do it for you the next time one blows.

☐ Look up an article on microfilm or microfiche (by using *Readers' Guide*) on a subject pertaining to your class to get the experience of using these machines.

☐ Check out a book to read for fun or for a book report.

☐ Work on a display for your class to put in the library display cases.

☐ Use the *Readers' Guide* to find magazine articles to supplement classroom materials.

☐ Learn to cover your paperback textbooks with contact paper.

☐ Use our career information to find out about jobs in your subject area.

☐ Practice a speech or a reading in our audiovisual room.

☐ Take a test he has missed.

☐ Study for a test while your students are going over the test the student missed.

☐ Do some research on how to make a movie and practice using the movie or video camera. (Then he or she can help you with filming.)

☐ Learn how to mend your worn books so they will last for the rest of the year.

☐ Watch or listen to any audiovisual presentation missed because of absence.

☐ Look at the film catalogs to locate a film that could be used in your class so that we may order it for you.

☐ Learn to operate the computer that is housed in the library, or use it to type a composition.

☐ Use the microfiche machine to secure information on various colleges.

☐ Do remedial or supplementary work by using the computer.

☐ Learn to do the letters for your bulletin board by using a computer program.

☐ Make up a crossword puzzle or word search game by using the computer. This product can then be used in your class if you give the student suggestions on subject matter.

☐ Use the slide maker to make slides for a program to be used for class or for open house.

☐ Use the student typewriters.

☐ Look over the television schedule for the week to see if there are any programs that would be good to show in your classroom.

☐ Come to the library to get acquainted if he is a new student or has missed his library orientation for some reason.

Dian Zillner is a high school librarian in Maryville, Missouri. This article was originally published in THE BOOK REPORT, November/December, 1984.

68 Ways To Catch A Teacher
By Helen F. Flowers

The initial step in curriculum involvement is to work with teachers on ways to integrate library activities into their teaching plans. Unfortunately, not all teachers are eager to include the librarian in their planning. What is required here is what I will term a pre-initial step—"catching a teacher."

Those teachers who are already users of the media center come in for planning or whatever services they need. Although they may be led to expand their use of the library, it is those who seldom come in who are the focus of interest here. My aim is (1) to get them into the library environment, (2) speak to them and show them at least one item, and (3) sell them on the idea of letting me team up with them on planning their lessons and assignments.

Some of the ways I have successfully attracted teachers, singly or in groups, are:

- ☐ Provide a pot of hot water and tea, instant coffee, and instant soup.
- ☐ Give teachers first chance at discarded books.
- ☐ Have the best pencil sharpener in school, an electric one if possible.
- ☐ Get the photocopier in the library.
- ☐ Notify teachers when you are ready to discard collections of old magazines.
- ☐ Get a typewriter, even an old one, for teacher use.
- ☐ Provide typing paper and correction liquid or tape.
- ☐ Volunteer to let students do make-up tests in the library.
- ☐ Make yesterday's newspaper available for clipping.
- ☐ Provide a home to the transparency maker.
- ☐ Supply write-on film and pens.
- ☐ Let student assistants make photocopies of materials teachers leave to pick up later.
- ☐ Scan magazines for articles of interest to particular teachers and ask them to stop by for their copies.
- ☐ Keep construction paper on hand.
- ☐ Provide sets of letter patterns in various sizes.
- ☐ Make available colored felt-tip markers for posters.
- ☐ Keep a pile of old magazines for clipping.
- ☐ Have a clip art collection.
- ☐ Make lists of gift book ideas for holidays.
- ☐ Send book reviews to teachers.
- ☐ Provide some popular adult fiction (costs money but pays off).

- ☐ Buy some titles from the best-seller list.
- ☐ Invite the principal to hold faculty meetings in the library. Be sure to display materials.
- ☐ Ask department chairmen to meet in the library and to give you some time on the agenda.
- ☐ Hold pot luck or brown bag luncheons in the library on teacher conference days. Exhibit materials.
- ☐ Ask teachers to come in to preview software.
- ☐ Ask teachers to suggest titles for purchase.
- ☐ Seek advice from teachers on weeding.
- ☐ Volunteer to cover a teacher's book with a clear plastic cover.
- ☐ Allow a teacher's unscheduled class to meet in the library in an emergency.
- ☐ Send holiday greetings and list holiday craft books on display.
- ☐ Maintain a file of information on education courses offered at nearby colleges.
- ☐ Keep information on inservice courses.
- ☐ Salvage things from your junk mail for teachers.
- ☐ Keep a file of information on prizes, awards, and grants.
- ☐ Notify individual teachers of upcoming television programs of interest to them.
- ☐ Get on a mailing list to receive discount tickets to plays, concerts, cultural events.
- ☐ Post information about exhibits at museums.
- ☐ Put student assistants in charge of the discount coupon file.
- ☐ Ask the teachers' association to use the library as its information center in the building.
- ☐ Ask the central office for a copy of the district policy handbook for teachers' use.
- ☐ Keep a copy of the teachers' contract.
- ☐ House the building's laminator.
- ☐ Let the student assistants make tapes of teachers' recordings.
- ☐ Keep road maps and maps of the local area.
- ☐ Order and file tourist kits from various states and foreign countries.
- ☐ Add vacation planning books to the collection.
- ☐ Keep information about hotel discount plans.
- ☐ Order freebies and make them available.
- ☐ Send copies of appropriate cartoons to teachers.
- ☐ Display examples of teachers' hobbies.
- ☐ Do a display of photographs of teachers as babies or kids.
- ☐ Ask a teacher to do a display case with you (i.e., display garments from sewing class along with books on sewing).

☐ Provide income tax preparation guides.

☐ Volunteer to plant sit over the summer or holidays if you are working then.

☐ Display student projects.

☐ Send out birthday greetings, notes of congratulations, sympathy notes, get well cards.

☐ Send books to teachers' mailboxes.

☐ Notify teachers of new book titles of interest to them.

☐ Distribute a "How Can I Help You" list of services.

☐ Keep a file of all building and district newsletters and other publications.

☐ Bind and catalog class newspapers and collections of writing.

☐ Collect colorful, funny, up-to-date posters for teachers to borrow.

☐ Mention teachers' names in your reports to administrators. Send copies to faculty.

☐ Prepare short, quick-to-read reports on library activities and distribute to teachers.

☐ Invite teachers to attend meetings of library organizations when programs would be of interest to them.

☐ Work on building social committees and invite them to hold meetings in the library.

☐ Invite teachers to attend materials fairs with you.

Helen Flowers has many years experience as a library media specialist at Bay Shore (New York) High School. A version of this article was originally published in THE BOOK REPORT, November/December 1984.

The Best Laid Plans and All That...
By Augie E. Beasley and Carolyn G. Palmer

Well-planned inservice workshops are among the best ways to tell teachers about the library's potential. Here are tips for making these workshops or any professional meeting more effective.

Facilities & Equipment
If you are unfamiliar with the building, tour it before the meeting. Notice electrical outlets and lighting capabilities. If there are few outlets, plan to bring several bar power sources. Of course, you must beware of overloading circuits. If you are in doubt, ask. When you look at the lighting, determine whether it can be dimmed for slides. If not, consider providing pen lights for speakers. Slides are ineffective in a bright room, but in a completely dark room speakers may need some light to see their notes.

The arrangements for table discussions can make them either effective or impossible. If there are too many groups in one large room, noise drowns out the discussion leaders. Putting too many people at one table is also a problem. Leave plenty of distance between tables. Use two large rooms or several small rooms, and assign only one topic per table.

Well in advance of a workshop ask speakers for a list of audiovisual equipment they will need. Then check—and double check—to see that equipment is in place and in good repair. Put an extra bulb in each meeting room and have someone present who knows how to change it. Different brands of equipment work differently, and speakers often do not know how to set up slides or videos. If videos are to be used, put up a monitor with a large screen. In a large room provide several monitors. If a public address system is being used, it must be audible in every part of the room. Check for clear sound and make necessary corrections before the presentation.

Speakers
Select speakers with reputations for lively, interesting presentations. Consult your state's education agency for suggestions of speakers from another region of the state. If several speakers are conducting a presentation and they are not accustomed to working together, have them agree on speaking order and allotted time in advance of the meeting. You may wish to provide someone for each session who will introduce the speakers and assist with preparations. Secure biographical data in advance. Have a pitcher of water and drinking glasses for speakers.

Impress on your speakers the need to be succinct and fast-paced. It is better to leave a group wanting more than to carry on so long that the participants begin shaking their watches.

The Session

Get the attention of participants with catchy titles for meetings. Write enticing annotations to increase interest. Of course, never oversell a speaker or a presentation.

Supply good handouts, visual aids, and other supplementary materials. Visual aids should be large enough for the audience to see plainly. You should also encourage speakers to display slides, videos, or well-designed transparencies before and after the meeting. Many of us are called media specialists, yet we often forget to use supplementary media (or worse, we misuse them). Handouts are essential. (We always feel cheated if a good handout isn't provided.) Good choices are bibliographies or instructions for activities.

The proper length for inservice sessions depends on the circumstances. If the meetings are held at the end of a school day, keep them short. One hour may suffice, if you plan a thin margin of optional extra time. If participants earn renewal credit, the length of inservices sessions must accord with state guidelines. (Do offer renewal credit when possible.) If you plan a whole inservice day, schedule 45-50 minutes for each presentation and open the day with a large group meeting.

Keep topics practical. The most popular sessions are full of good ideas and handouts. Some participants complain that they already know the tricks of the trade; nevertheless, experience has taught us that practical workshops are the best received.

Consider the size of groups when you plan the meetings. Some presentations lend themselves to large groups, but most workshop sessions can best accommodate no more than 20 participants. If 50 or more attend, schedule several sessions. Participants may move from session to session, so you must label the meeting sites well and supply maps or directions. Rest rooms must also appear in directions and on maps.

Meeting Management

Publish information about a conference early, including presentation titles and the names of speakers. Anticipate problems and devise solutions in advance (what if a speaker cannot come, a scheduled room cannot be used, or the weather doesn't cooperate?).

Here is a solution to the problem of helpers—invite a school club or athletic team to assist with parking cars, loading materials, and helping speakers. You should also keep carts and hand trucks available for moving speakers' materials.

And of course, wear comfortable shoes and keep your sense of humor.

For many years Augie Beasley & the late Carolyn Palmer were a media specialist team at East Mecklenburg High School, North Carolina. A version of this article was originally published in THE BOOK REPORT, November/December 1988.

Design Basics
By Marilyn Fredrickson & Jane Cabaya

An art teacher and a librarian share their "rules" for bulletin board and display designs.

Bulletin board and display ideas come easily if you are constantly on the lookout for layouts and designs. You'll find many ideas and themes that can be adapted for your library displays in newspapers, magazines, and advertising brochures. Holidays are an especially good time to find colorful and catchy ideas in magazines and greeting cards. (Remember, of course, you are seeking ideas not reproducing work protected by copyrights.)

Simplicity is the most basic rule for any display. One strong theme or slogan should deliver your message. It should be displayed without clutter so that it can be read and understood at a glance. The amount of time you expect people to look at your display is proportional to how much detail you will present. A fast look demands a simple display with eye-catching colors and short information. Simple and short should also be the rule for displays for a "trapped audience" of students and teachers.

Be sure to tailor the message to the reading level of your audience. Adults might be attracted to hidden or subtle meaning but young children require a straightforward message.

Color, in contrasting and bright shades, helps catch the eye; however, just a splash of bright color on a neutral background can create a center of interest.

Background should be just what the word implies. It should not compete with the lettering or the illustrations. Many different types of materials may be used—from wallpaper and cardboard to styrofoam and wood, table cloths and bolts of fabric. Even old curtains may prove useful.

If visuals are needed in the background, it is much easier to cut out representative shapes than to draw them. Geometric shapes can be used to simplify objects and, also, add interesting stylized effects. Unique effects can be achieved with origami—folding heavy paper into shapes to represent buildings, animals, and people.

Lettering may be simple or complicated depending on your abilities or access to tools such as stencils and mechanical lettering sets. If you are good at drawing letters for bulletin boards, a catalog from a press-on lettering company will be a useful guide.

Make your art and lettering work together. Old style letters will not do much for a space-age science display. Lettering can "speak" loudly if you display some important words in all capital letters, or use no capital letters in your captions. Using a contrasting color or a different texture for one or more words can also make those words stand out. Yarn, rope or wire can be quickly fashioned into cursive letters. However, avoid narrow letters than cannot be read at a distance.

Don't spread letters so far apart that it is difficult for viewers to read your message. Keep words in one area of the bulletin board or display so the message is easily apparent.

Display materials can be found in the oddest places—junk shops—junk shops, art stores, department stores, farmyards, lumberyards, grocery stores, and sales. Scraps of tagboard, carpet, old paneling, styrofoam sheets, big pieces of cloth, boxes, and children's toys offer promise. Of course, you will have to reserve a storage space for all the "junk" you will collect.

Weight and height are major factors to consider in choosing display materials. Bicycle hooks, cup hooks, Velcro, paper clips and string, fish line and wire, all have their place in your inventory. Glues, rubber cement, and starches are old standbys but each has its own specific properties. Be sure you follow directions for liquid adhesives so you do not damage objects used in your displays. Styrofoam, sponges, and balsa wood are lightweight materials that can seem to be suspended in space if attached to a wire or thread. Another method for giving the illusion of a suspension is to fasten an object to a small box and then attach the hidden box to the wall.

When time is short, create your bulletin board right before your viewers' eyes. Regular visitors might enjoy watching the display grow.

Art teacher Marilyn Frederickson and librarian Jane Cabaya teamed up at the Kasson-Mantorville Schools in Kasson, Minnesota. A version of this article was originally published in THE BOOK REPORT, January/February 1989.

Infinite Bibliographies
Tailor-made Guides Good for the Life of the Unit in Any Library
By Joanne R. Stewart

After observing students locked into author-title bibliographies, the author designed a guide that will lead students to pertinent research sources in any library, any time. The good part is, these bibliographies don't need to be updated or revised as the collection changes.

There are basically two kinds of assignments that bring students to the library: (1) a book report, in which the student must select one book, read it, and make some sort of report on it; and (2) an information gathering assignment, in which the student must locate, digest and present material about some subject. In this case, many resources should be explored and investigated. Portions of books are simply one of the possibilities. This kind of assignment may or may not require the student to make a list of the sources he used, or identify whose ideas he is discussing. Obviously, the ultimate "information gathering" assignment for a high school student is a term or research paper.

The Limitations Of Author-Title Bibliographies

The standard author-title bibliography is helpful to students doing book report assignments, but somewhat less helpful to students doing information-gathering assignments. People are comfortable with these lists and have come to accept them, traditionally, as the only way to proceed. I submit that they are not the only way, and that there are real drawbacks and limitations to them.

First, no matter how careful and thorough the preparation, there will always be omissions. It is impossible to include everything that ought to be included. Second, materials that are not available at all are often on author-title lists. They may be long out-of-print or not available in the community from any source. Third, as new materials become available they are not on the lists. To overcome these limitations, continuous revision, publication and distribution would be necessary.

The Concept Is Born

What device could be developed that would provide the needed assistance for students while at the same time avoiding the limitations of a traditional author-title bibliography? The obvious answer was to provide students with appropriate subject headings instead of a list of books. Over the years this idea was reinforced in my mind as I watched students standing in front of the card catalog or the *Readers' Guide,* assignment in hand on a faded ditto, not know what to look up. They couldn't come up with that entry word which would open up the world of resources at hand. The teachers, too, had this same problem and could not be of much help to their students, although they tried. It was the librarian who had studied and applied cataloging theory, who knew how subject headings were constructed and what they meant. This was the kind of information that needed to be transmitted to teachers and students, even to those already possessing good routine library skills. And we also had to reach those who did not possess adequate library skills.

Working with teachers who were receptive to the concept, our library staff has developed many "infinite bibliographies" or reading guides. They have been used for several years now with great success. Some have been keyed to particular textbooks, but most have not. It is an extremely flexible tool and can be adapted to any class level in any content area. It can cover an entire course, a grading period, or simply one unit of work. It deals with all forms of materials. It can be combined with an modest author-title bibliography if desired. There don't seem to be any major drawbacks to the idea in fact.

We have also developed modified infinite bibliographies intended solely for use with the *Readers' Guide*, at the request of several teachers. These, too, are proving highly satisfactory in use. We hope to continue moving in this direction and improve the concept as we go along.

Preparing the Bibliography

In an ideal teacher-librarian cooperation model, the teacher presents his assignment to the librarian for a feasibility check. During a conference, the librarian finds out (a) the teacher's objectives, (b) the grade level and intellectual ability of the students, (c) the number of students, (d) the time, (e) the specific content, and (f) the need for library skills instruction.

Usually within a day or two, the librarian determines if the research can be carried out with the resources at hand, or with modifications. Then the librarian prepares an infinite bibliography for the assignment. The teacher makes the final decision, incorporating the librarian's suggestions. Several advantages are obvious.

1. There is absolutely no threat to the teacher's professionalism, status, or authority. Classroom teachers are sometimes insecure about this. The librarian is functioning as a true resource person.
2. The teacher knows in advance that the assignment is possible in the local setting and that students will be able to succeed.
3. The public library can easily be alerted to the assignment and sent copies of both the infinite bibliography and the assignment. Both school and public library staffs will be ready to cope with students doing the assignment.

4. Weaknesses in the collection are discovered.
5. The librarian can make the necessary procedural decisions in advance; e.g., shorten the loan period for titles not in sufficient number for the number of students involved.

Once a teacher has tried the concept and discovered how well it works, trust and rapport are developed between that teacher and the librarian. Everyone is better off, especially the students—and this, after all, is the bottom line.

Samples of two bibliographies appear in boxed copy at the end of this article. "Ancient Classical History" was prepared for a freshman social studies curriculum, called the History of World Civilization. The history course is offered in nine-week units in several ways. One sequence calls for units titled Emergence of Man, Ancient Classical History, the Middle Ages and the Renaissance, and Search for Survival. Another sequence is composed of studies of areas such as China and Japan, the Middle East, Latin America and so forth. We have prepared infinite bibliographies for each of these units.

In a typical first assignment requiring the use of library materials, the student might be instructed to find one book in the card catalog which might be useful in this class and write a bibliography entry. Additional assignments are usually one book report and one short information-gathering piece with a list of sources used. The entire class is usually scheduled into the library to do the first assignment. At that time the infinite bibliography is introduced by the librarian. Subsequent assignments are done by the students on their own time. (The freshmen receive an orientation to the library in the first few weeks of their English classes. The social studies teachers wait until the orientation is completed before they give their first research assignments.)

The infinite bibliography for consumer education (see boxed copy) came about because a teacher was frustrated in his attempts to assign newspaper and magazine reference work to his students. "These kids not only don't know anything about business and economics, they don't even know newspapers exist! Can't we do anything?" he fumed.

I assured him we could do a great deal. From his assignment I could see that he wanted his students to become aware that business, economics and consumer matters were important daily news, just as politics, crime, and sports were. During our conference I confirmed his objectives and scheduled his class into the library for two consecutive days. Then I prepared the infinite bibliography. During the first session, we reviewed the assignment and the infinite bibliography. The next day the students began their work under the supervision of their teacher and the library staff. The teacher was ecstatic about the infinite bibliography (and even told the principal how marvelous he thought it was).

An infinite bibliography is a reference and research tool, with a sound theoretical basis, prepared by the professional school librarian in consultation with a classroom teacher. It is intended to assist students in doing their school assignments with dispatch, in a productive and systematic manner. It is a simple, logical concept that has proved highly successful in actual use. It teaches reference methods with a content focus, and reinforces any previous library skills introduction.

For optimum success, it should be introduced to the class by the librarian and, as the students' work progresses, should be supervised both by the librarian and by the teacher, working in tandem. The tool has all the advantages of the traditional author-title bibliography and none of the disadvantages. When it is properly prepared, introduced and utilized, it is much more helpful and efficient in achieving the desired results than the traditional bibliography.

Joanne Stewart made infinite bibliographies as the head librarian for the Waukegan, Illinois, East High School. A version of this article was originally published in THE BOOK REPORT, September/October 1985.

Consumer Education Research Methods

1. *Readers' Guide to Periodical Literature*
   Articles of interest to students of consumer education appear in many
   magazines. Among them:

Atlantic	Nation
Business Week	National Review
Changing Times	Nation's Business
Congressional Digest	New Republic
Consumer Reports	Newsweek
Consumers' Research	Progressive
Current	Society
Environment	Time
Forbes	U.S. News and World Report
Fortune	Vital Speeches
Harper's	

The school library subscribes to all of these and they are also indexed
by subject in the *Readers' Guide*.

Suggested subject headings to use:

BANKS AND BANKING	INTEREST (ECONOMICS)
ECONOMIC FORECASTING	INVESTMENTS
ECONOMIC INDICATORS	SUPPLY AND DEMAND
INFLATION (FINANCE)	U.S. — ECONOMIC POLICY

2. Card Catalog. Suggested subject headings to find books and filmstrips:
   CONSUMER EDUCATION
   INFLATION (FINANCE)
   TAXATION
   U.S. — ECONOMIC CONDITIONS (divided by date)
   U.S. — ECONOMIC POLICY

3. Pamphlet File. Suggested subject headings:
   INFLATION (FINANCE)
   U.S. — ECONOMIC CONDITIONS
   U.S. — ECONOMIC POLICY

4. Don't forget newspapers! Most have business sections.

Chicago Defender	New York Times (Sunday)
Chicago Sun-Times	News-Sun
Chicago Tribune	U.S.A. Today
	Wall Street Journal

5. Suggested reference books

   R
   300 Encyclopedia of social sciences
   E

   R
   310 Information please almanac
   I

   R
   310 World Almanac
   W

   R
   317.3 Statistical abstract of the United States
   U

   R
   328.73 Congress and the nation
   C

   R
   330.03 Dictionary of business and economics
   A

   R
   330.3 McGraw-Hill dictionary of modern economics
   M

   R
   330.3 Paradis, Economics reference book
   8

Ancient Classical History

1. Words to know and understand.

   biography   subject heading   e.g.
   collective   subdivision   etc.
   individual   call number   antiquity
                                          classical

2. People. To find collective and individual biographies (920 and 921)

   a. Use a person's name as a subject heading, e.g. CAESAR, CAIUS JULIUS; ARISTOTLE, to locate information.

   b. Use any subject heading with the subdivision — BIOGRAPHY, e.g., ROME-BIOGRAPHY, to locate books about people related to that subject.

3. Names and places, used alone or with subdivisions, are good subject headings, e.g., EGYPT; EGYPT-HISTORY; EGYPT-KINGS AND RULERS

4. Literary Works.

   Novels and Short Stories. Look for the subdivision. —FICTION. e.g., GREECE-FICTION; HANNIBAL-FICTION. Then look at the call number. In our library 808.3 means short stories, and the author's last initial only means the book is a novel.

   Poetry and Drama.
   Use the name of the writer as author, e.g., Plato
   Use the name of the writer as subject, e.g., PLATO
   Use LATIN LITERATURE; GREEK DRAMA; GREEK LITERATURE and the literary subdivision —COLLECTIONS; —HISTORY AND CRITICISM

5. Brush up on the parts of a catalog card

   913.32   EGYPT-CIVILIZATION—TO 332 B.C.
      S   Silverberg, Robert
              Before the sphinx; early Egypt
           Nelson, c1971
              176p.

6. Summary

   a. Use names of people and places as your subject. Be careful about time periods (913's and 930's)

   b. Watch for helpful subdivisions of major subject headings.

      —ANTIQUITIES   —FICTION   —POLITICS AND GOVERNMENT
      —BIOGRAPHY   —HISTORY   —SOCIAL LIFE AND CUSTOMS
      —CIVILIZATION   —KINGS AND RULERS

   c. Consider also for use as subject headings

      ARCHITECTURE, GREEK   MYTHOLOGY, CLASSICAL
      ARCHITECTURE, ROMAN   PHILOSOPHY, GREEK
      CIVILIZATION, GREEK   SCULPTURE, GREEK

   d. Our library uses ALL CAPITAL LETTERS to identify a subject card. The Public Library uses red tape. All libraries use one or the other of these devices so you can quickly recognize a subject card.

   e. All possible subject headings cannot be included here. You will be able to think of and use others, and you should do this.

7. Suggested Reference Books

   R
   291 Evans. Dictionary of mythology.
   E

   R
   291 Grimal. Larousse world mythology.
   G

   R
   292 Tripp. Crowell's handbook of classical mythology.
   T

   R
   703 Praeger encyclopedia of art. 5v.
   P

Online Serendipity
By Margaret J. Schmude

We began teaching online searching by making it part of the English classes' research unit. The unit was built around a review of standard research skills plus some new techniques, all aimed at writing a research paper. We gave students time to begin their research and toward the end of the unit, I introduced online searching. I began the unit by talking about the sheer volume of information available and the impossibility of wading through it with traditional research techniques. We spent time on the concept of searching, its benefits, the development of a search strategy, the actual execution of the search, and how to use the information it yields.

This supposedly computer-wise generation had difficulty visualizing online searching and its results. I used transparencies and examples of actual searches, but the real break-through came when students sat at the computer and saw the program working on their research problems. At the blackboard we worked together to design search strategies for their individual topics. I emphasized the use of the Boolean operators AND, OR, and NOT in search statements. These are "arguments" that combine simple search elements into compound searches. The student searches for all the books written by, say, Asimov AND all books written in 1986. As the students found out, these compound searches can be impressively specific. Sometimes, of course, the search is too specific, and no data are retrieved.

After discussing search strategies, I had each student schedule a time to execute a search. At first, the students relied on *Magazine Index,* but they soon became more adventuresome and began using other indexes such as *Newsweek, Sport,* and *Smoking and Health.* Of course, that created our next problem: how to obtain the books and magazines cited in the databases. Our collection could supply only some of the materials. The public library came to our aid with the interlibrary loan service—and a cooperative spirit.

Students soon discovered that they could use information from article abstracts—a rather sophisticated discovery for high school students. In fact, abstracts became a popular way to retrieve information since they were brief and to the point. In addition, the students learned how to cite abstracts in their bibliographies, another new skill.

At that point, the teachers and I began to refine our techniques and expand into other domains. Two of the major successes were in advanced placement classes in American government and in English.

Online in the Classroom
The government assignment was to write a position paper. The teacher and I developed a list of topics having to do with the rights of

individuals — smokers' rights, the legal definition of death, child abuse, and so forth. The English-and-speech teacher helped teach the correct format for a position paper.

Because many of these students had been introduced to online searching in their English classes, we could add more sophisticated search terms and use some of the more advanced features of the DIALOG program. We discussed the use of the EXPAND command, how to limit information by publication year, and how to selected the format in which the material is received. Students discovered that truncating words and phrases helped them find more information. They used the OR command more.

Students were also more willing to venture into new databases. They began using *Environline, Middle East Abstracts, Criminal Justice Periodicals Index* and *Child Abuse and Neglect.*

With the government class, we had fewer problems in tracking down the sources. The public library reported that many students arrived there with printouts in hand. And they knew how to located holdings in other libraries, often traveling to those libraries to get the materials they needed.

The advanced placement English project used cooperative learning groups to explore philosophical and historical aspects of Dostoyevsky's *Crime and Punishment.* By this time, students were so accustomed to the technique of online searching that many came to the library immediately. We found that developing search strategies by committee yielded unexpected rewards. The selection of search terms was unusually rich and varied. The selection of databases followed the same trend, getting us into *MLA Bibliography, Arts and Humanities Search, Biography Index, Philosopher's Index, Religion Index* and *Historical Abstracts,* to name a few.

Students also accepted that they would have to go outside our small library for many of the materials they needed. However, this time the teacher made it easy for them. She arranged a field trip to a university library.

Serendipity

Although we expected to expand our students' research skills, online searching yielded some unexpected benefits. For example,

- Online searching proved to be one of the best critical thinking exercises offered to our students. They were forced to think their projects through, to narrow topics, to brainstorm, and to know what they were looking for before they went near the computer. The process of searching changed students' hypotheses and shaped their ideas. Researching became a lively, recursive process that, in may instances, took precedence over the final product.

- Students learned to appreciate the meaning of the term "information explosion" when they found 12,234 articles on abortion in one database.
- Online searching forced students to begin using sources outside their school and public libraries. They began to see how different libraries emphasize different subjects and materials. Many said that it broadened their outlook on the research process and sharpened their researching skills.
- Teachers reported that their students had become fascinated with the research process. It became a living thing, which caused lively exchanges among group members.
- Online search changed the teachers' attitude toward research as a teaching tool. In fact, the students quickly outstripped their teachers in the development of online skills. Teachers began asking for workshops; they found more ways to make the development of research skills part of their teaching.

Some Do's and Don'ts

- *Do enlist the support of the teachers.* Begin on a small scale, with one teacher or class. Offer to teach the process in their classrooms. Coach the teachers in online skills. They will soon see how the process can benefit their students.
- *Do alert the public library and enlist the staff's support in helping students obtain materials.* Our library has been invaluable in providing interlibrary loan and central serials service.
- *Do integrate online searching into the body of research skills and direct the teaching toward a specific project.* Students are able to see immediate benefits when search skills are directed to their own assignments.
- *Don't expect instant understanding.* The concept of online searching is a difficult one for many students (and teachers) to grasp.
- *Do make sure that students are familiar with traditional research techniques before beginning an online project.* They must understand that different databases use different subject headings.
- *Don't let students near the computer until they have a general understanding of the topic.* Spend a few days in traditional research so that students can become familiar with the subject they will be researching.
- *Do take time to review the search strategy with the individual students or group of students before going online.* This is a good point at which to check their understanding of both the topic and the concept of online searching.

- *Do encourage students to try different databases and advanced techniques.* The tendency for many is to stick with indexes that seem familiar.
- *Don't limit the teaching online searching to one subject.* We began in English, went to social studies, and are hoping to expand to project in science, art and music, business and foreign language. The more students see online searching's benefits in all parts of the curriculum, the more likely they are to see how different topics are related.

Margaret Schmude has experience as the head of Instructional Media services at Zion-Benton Township High School, Zion, Illinois. A version of this article was originally published in THE BOOK REPORT, September/October 1989.

Staying in the Kitchen
Notes on a Censorship Battle
By Edna M. Boardman

A veteran of an eight-year ideological cold war shares some of what she learned along with practical advice for weathering censorship attempts.

My doctor listened patiently as I reeled off a list of stress-related symptoms: dizziness, irregular heartbeat, indigestion, and an incredible inner tension. His eyes narrowed. "If you can't stand the heat," he said, "get out of the kitchen."

My community of 30,000 (whose schools also educate children from a nearby SAC base) was in the middle of a hard-fought school board election. I reacted with my stomach every time library books were mentioned—and they were mentioned often.

Censorship wars, I learned, are not for the psychologically fragile, and ultimately I spent eight years battling over the books in the school libraries. My doctor's words helped me muster the toughness I would need to survive it all.

Some of the old, bad feelings return as I look through my fat collection of clippings. Here is a sampling.

"...every book coming into the schools' libraries should be reviewed in advance to determine its literary value and readability and to 'see if it accomplished the fact that it will make the child a better person.'"—The Minot Daily News, *February 2, 1978.*

"We state categorically that there is no general anxiety with current library practices among patrons of the Minot Public School System. Only one formal Request for Reconsideration has ever been received within the entire system, and none of us has ever received negative comments off the record."—Position paper composed by the district school librarians, March 29, 1979.

"I can't understand how anyone would object to someone trying to ensure that the books our children read are good influences and not harmful. Kids are bombarded everywhere with literature more likely to produce moral cripples than build sound character. Does America benefit or deteriorate as a result?"—*Letter to the editor,* The Minot Daily News, *March 31, 1979.*

"The board also voted unanimously to seek legal advice about the ramifications of a law which [a school board member] asserted made it necessary that all such materials be reviewed under penalty of loss of funding." — The Minot Daily News, *February 15, 1980.*

"[A School Board Member] announced her committee after she voted against the 1984-85 budget, which provided $98,000 for library books. She then proceeded to check out numerous books from various school libraries, and also search for specific titles from the checklist of 60 books which she still refuses to divulge. 'This was not book reviewing. This was an investigative report,' [she] said. 'I wanted to determine how you could select $98,000 work of library books without anyone reading them first. I wanted to see what kinds of books we get for $98,000 when selected in a lottery fashion. It turns out you get some bad books when they're selected this way,' she said. 'The librarians are unwilling to admit that this blind throw-darts-at-at-the-booklist method is a mistake.'" — The Minot Daily News, *June 1, 1985.*

"Leave the Books Alone" — *Headline,* The Minot Daily News, *March 12, 1986. This was the first official editorial position ever taken by the local paper on this issue.*

Anyone who imagines that a censorship battle is a neat presentation of viewpoints followed by a clear-cut resolution of the issue is *wrong*. The controversy rambled on in our community with an unpredictable jumble of attacks on almost every decision related to books and the curriculum. The battle was fought in school board meetings and elections, on radio talk shows, in the local newspaper, in public forums, through letters, and on television. No orderly list of charges was ever made.

"Unpredictable" best describes the course of the controversy year-by-year. Here is just a sampling of incidents:

- I once received from a school board member a list of books to remove from my order. Five years later she said she had simply tagged many of them because they looked interesting and thought maybe she would enjoy reading them when they came in. Why, I wondered hadn't she told me that at the time? I had not, of course, removed them from my order in the first place.

- At one public forum before a spring school board election, a candidate read a dirty word list, purportedly from the *American Heritage Dictionary,* as indicative of what is in the books in our schools. The dictionaries had been removed from the desks of elementary teachers the previous November.

• During much of one school year, the school libraries were visited almost daily by members of a school board-parent committee checking out books for critical review. The card catalog, at one time, was checked and evaluated against a list we librarians were never permitted to see.

• We received national attention when the school board voted to eliminate classroom use of *Newsweek* because it was too liberal. (This vote was later rescinded.)

• An angry woman, who attended many school board meetings over a long period of time, rose to protest whenever she heard something she didn't like.

• Mel and Norma Gabler of Educational Research Analysis, the Texas-based textbook screen group, came to town at a time when the community mood was brittle. To our surprise they had a calming effect on the situation. They told our critics, "You have people there who are willing to work with you. Work with them."

• A school board member requested that the district order a biography of Phyllis Schlafly and give it to me for my library. When it arrived, I cataloged it and placed it on the shelf—beside the copy I already had.

• We were mentioned several times by the American Library Association's Office for Intellectual Freedom publication, *Newsletter for Intellectual Freedom.*

• When a social studies teacher arranged public sessions to show some slide sets that had been attacked, almost no one showed up.

• A teacher found a Time-Life book about evolution on a back shelf in an elementary school library with the words "Do Not Circulate" in big, black letters across the front.

• There were frequent efforts to lower the library book budget and instead spend money on take-home copies of textbooks. Once, a school board member suggested diverting book money to improve the city's hockey rink.

Grievances & Pressures

The school librarians in our district were accused of shoddy selection practices, undermining the moral fiber of the young, being insensitive to the values of our public and ignorant of the impact of our materials, pre-emptive censoring, promulgating inappropriate philosophies, deliberately removing excellent material, being "liberal," and more. It was impossible to predict what we would be accused of.

We were criticized because we shelved books without having first personally read them—something we librarians perceived to be a particularly frustrating game of "gotcha." Our critics did not see professional review as an appropriate substitute. (Indeed they refused to acknowledge the existence of professional review.) The fact that no profession functions on the isolated efforts and principles of its practitioners did not seem to count.

We had support, but not one person who contacted us from outside the Minot community understood the pressures we faced. University professors doing censorship-related research, intellectual freedom committees, journalists, and attorneys interested in intellectual freedom questions always assumed that specific materials already in our collection were being formally attacked. Specific titles came under fire a number of times, but removal of particular books was rarely the thrust of our critics. Rather, they pushed for a committee outside the normal school structure to review materials before purchase, as if preview by a citizen was the answer to all the ambiguities we deal with in selecting materials for young people. (We wondered if this demand was unique among communities with censorship battles.)

Part of the debate turned on the charge that we had much material of poor literary quality on our shelves. This charge was difficult to answer. Is an encyclopedia "material of poor literary quality"? What about a cookbook? Also, when we checked our collections against a list of classics provided by our critics we found we had almost all that were grade-appropriate.

Observations

Our critics never claimed to be part of an organization with a name. In effect, they resisted going through a process of filling out the Request for Reconsideration forms required by our district for removal of materials from the classrooms and libraries.

While all the libraries in the school system received some negative attention, mine, serving 11th and 12th grades, was most often cited as having offending materials. This may have been because, at the higher grades, we did shelve a greater range of materials. Or it may have been because I was the librarian most likely to push back publicly by speaking up at meetings or initiating position papers.

I was interviewed just once on television; I generally avoided interviews because I felt the reporters were seeking an emotional reaction.

Although we librarians were accused of "undermining youth," our work was much in the open. Students checked out thousands of books during the years of the controversy. Yet, little of the debate was generated by parentswho were disturbed by the books the children brought home from the libraries. Instead, a distinct minority sought control over selection.

Allegedly factual information about the collection or my manner of working rarely came from any contact with me or the library. I felt that my critics were not especially interested in what I thought or how I actually approached the selection process. But even when they did visit the library, they seemed to be seeking only scraps of support for their allegations.

Only a few students involved themselves in the controversy. Some spoke out, but most seemed to feel that the furor wasn't their concern. People on all sides of the issue, I think, acted responsibly in not especially recruiting students as partisans.

The religious affiliations of teachers and librarians were little different from those of their critics; however, "sides" did tend to align with churches in the community.

Some things I learned from the experience could be summarized thus:

Censorship battles are draining, and school people are right to want to avoid them. Lengthy battles create a polarizing, acrimonious atmosphere. Some community airing of views stimulates discussion and shows young people our heritage of freedom of thought and speech. But, too much battling can preoccupy teachers, librarians, and administrators, leading to self-censorship of all kinds. In wearing them out, the battle can also divert their energy from actually teaching.

Communication hinges on perspective. In our community, people simply did not interpret what they heard in the same way. If I heard the words *"Newsweek* has to go because it is too liberal," others heard "I'm here looking out for your interests; I'm defending your child against the ideas of the evil world out there."

It would have helped to talk with our critics, not just stand on principle, but the public arena in which the debate was carried out made this difficult. I felt my critics were more interested in stating their viewpoint that in hearing what I had to say. I suspect they felt the same way about me.

Most of the news media are only interested in today's events. In eight years there was considerable turnover among reporters, and only a few tried to understand the whole picture. They would listen to what was said *that day* and report it at face value. There were only two in-depth articles, one of which was in a magazine not normally read by the general public.

It is difficult for people who are genuinely disturbed by an open information system to have their wishes honored. I could not both shelve and keep off the shelves material expressing a variety of views. Also, I, as a librarian, was simply at an impasse. My freedom to operate a public school library and their freedom to selected preferred reading material were two incompatible concepts.

Not all book removals mean defeat. We librarians had to realize that removal of books through our written Request for Reconsideration process was not necessarily a failure. It is how our district's selection system is designed to work.

Some General, Free Advice

- Don't even think of running a library without a printed selection policy, complete with a Request for Reconsideration process. If your school board refuses to adopt such a policy, make it your library policy.

- Think about what you are doing. Frequently reread the "Library Bill of Rights" (ALA), but also develop a personal philosophy for your work. If you disagree with official positions taken by the national or state library associations, acknowledge these differences to yourself.

- While organizations will be there to give moral support, they probably will not be able to rescue you if the going truly gets tough.

- Document what happens. Have "visitor reports" in your file if critics visit your library. Jot down who visited or called, when, what they did, said, and looked at. Add anything you observed and how they made you feel. Such reports will help you remember the specifics of what really happened.

Some Words to Administrators

DO have clearly written philosophies, policies, and procedures on the materials used in your school's classrooms and libraries.

DO work with your librarians to develop a weeding policy. Don't lock them into a system that requires assembling a citizens' committee to discard a 15-year-old set of encyclopedias.

DO NOT distance yourself from your librarians and teachers under fire. Drawing some of the flack to yourself frees them to do their work. My administrators told me, "We believe you are doing an excellent job in a sensitive area. We know that, occasionally, you will make a mistake. When you do, we'll deal with it. We don't want you running scared." Their steady support helped me survive.

DO NOT make promises you cannot keep, such as promising someone to get rid of a book quietly. It will almost always become public, and it will hurt your credibility both with the public and with your staff.

Personal Survival for the Librarian

The attacks during a censorship battle can undermine your self-esteem. Coping with such a controversy, even for those determined to "stay in the kitchen," exacts a tremendous toll in time, energy, and spirit. (I did not realize how great a toll until the attacks finally subsided and I could again devote my full attention to my daily work. Where did all this new energy come from?) You can present your case, but it doesn't stay presented. Your critics may simply disagree or think you are lying anyhow. Here are some ways of coping I found helpful:

- Don't take things personally. Few if any will consider you to be the sole culprit.
- Develop a broad perspective. Realize this is not just personal battle. Some of the questions raised in our community were as old as books and libraries themselves. You are professionally trained to do what you are doing; you have been caught in the act of doing what you were hired to do. You have no authority to hand your professional prerogatives to anyone who demands them.
- Do not engage in shouting matches.
- Do not isolate yourself. Gather supportive, like-minded people around you.
- You don't have to respond to everything, either privately or publicly. After you've stated your position, smile a lot. It helps to lighten up and cultivate a sense of humor. It even helps to become a little cynical about it all.
- Talk about other subjects when you are with family and friends, or you increasingly become personally identified with the issue. After a while, little new can be said. If you are tagged as argumentative or a one-issue talker, you might seem boring to others.

- Take a vacation; practice relaxation techniques; take a break from the news. (I found most of my solace and support at my church.)

How It Ended

The controversy has eased, or at least gone underground. It most assuredly was not resolved by one side changing the other or "winning." A fine, private, religious elementary school was opened, helping those parents who couldn't come to terms with a public school's policies.

I think the community got tired of the battle; they eventually elected new people to the school board. The new members, representative of all parts of the community, changed the focus of what was debated in the meetings and in the media.

Edna Boardman is the library media specialist at the Magic City Campus of the Minot, North Dakota, High School. This article was in issue of THE BOOK REPORT, November/December 1989.